The Fellas:
Overcoming Prison
and Addiction

CHARLES M. TERRY
St. Louis University

WADSWORTH
—★—™
THOMSON LEARNING

Australia • Canada • Mexico • Singapore • Spain
United Kingdom • United States

WADSWORTH

THOMSON LEARNING™

Senior Executive Editor, Criminal Justice:
Sabra Horne
Assistant Editor: Dawn Mesa
Editorial Assistant: Paul Massicotte
Technology Project Manager: Susan DeVanna
Marketing Manager: Dory Schaeffer
Marketing Assistant: Neena Chandra
Advertising Project Manager: Stacey Purviance
Project Manager, Editorial Production:
Matt Ballantyne

Print/Media Buyer: Judy Inouye
Permissions Editor: Sarah Harkrader
Production Service: Forbes Mill Press
Copy Editor: Robin Gold
Cover Designer: Yvo Riezebos
Compositor: Forbes Mill Press
Cover Image: Punchstock
Text and Cover Printer: Webcom

Printed in Canada
1 2 3 4 5 6 7 06 05 04 03 02

For more information about our products,
contact us at:
Thomson Learning Academic Resource Center
1-800-423-0563

For permission to use material from this text,
contact us by:
Phone: 1-800-730-2214   **Fax:** 1-800-730-2215
Web: http://www.thomsonrights.com

Library of Congress Control Number
2002115050

ISBN 0-534-59904-4

Wadsworth/Thomson Learning
10 Davis Drive
Belmont, CA 94002-3098
USA

Asia
Thomson Learning
5 Shenton Way #01-01
UIC Building
Singapore 068808

Australia/New Zealand
Thomson Learning
102 Dodds Street
Southbank, Victoria 3006
Australia

Canada
Nelson
1120 Birchmount Road
Toronto, Ontario M1K 5G4
Canada

Europe/Middle East/Africa
Thomson Learning
High Holborn House
50/51 Bedford Row
London WC1R 4LR
United Kingdom

Latin America
Thomson Learning
Seneca, 53
Colonia Polanco
11560 Mexico D.F.
Mexico

Spain
Paraninfo Thomson Learning
Calle/Magallanes, 25
28015 Madrid, Spain

Contents

Preface

The ideological underpinnings of the "War on Drugs" helped produce and justify the unprecedented swelling of the prison population in the United States during the past two decades. As never before, addicts have been and continue to be incarcerated—often for long periods, typically for nonviolent crimes. To varying degrees, this policy creates people who see themselves and their worlds from the perspective of both an addict *and* a convict. Each is highly stigmatized in the wider culture. Each has crippling, alienating effects for how we see ourselves is a reflection of how we are seen by others.

The Fellas is a story about the struggle of overcoming the effects of heroin addiction and incarceration. Based on the life histories of 20 men, it provides a means of understanding the social forces and situations that can lead people into and away from lifestyles that center around the chronic use of drugs and imprisonment.

My interest in writing this book stemmed from my own experiences as an addict and a convict that spanned a period of roughly 20 years. The roads the fellas have taken are similar to many I have traveled myself. Throughout the text, I intersperse snapshots from my own life to clarify specific concepts or set up a particular segment of their stories.

The first two chapters introduce the fellas, provide the theoretical backdrop of the book, and place them within a historical context by summarizing the social construction of addict images dating back to the mid-19th century. The rest of the book is about their differences and similarities, their experiences in prison and out, and what they did to turn their lives around.

The Fellas is an honest, straightforward representation of a social world most people have ideas about but few really understand. Unlike most criminological research, it is an attempt to capture the pain, suffering, courage, and compassion that are at the heart of the human condition. It is my sincerest hope that as these pages are read, people will recognize these feelings in themselves and, in turn, be able to empathize not only with "addicts" and "convicts," but with all human beings just a little bit more than they could before reading the book.

Acknowledgments

I wish to thank everyone who helped make this book possible. Although listing all their names is impossible, I feel compelled to begin by expressing my deepest gratitude to all my family members who have always been there for me—no matter what. Even though things came between some of us at times, our love and support for one another never really died. For that I am truly grateful.

A heartfelt thanks to my two greatest mentors on this project: Paul Jesilow and Tom Shibutani. Paul, relentless in his critique about the quality, organization, and clarity of my writing, taught me more than he'll ever know. His availability and calm, encouraging demeanor enhanced not only my scholastic ability but also my confidence. Once a week for many months I met with Tom, a renowned authority on the relationship between identity and behavior, for breakfast. During our meetings, he taught me invaluable information that helped this book take shape.

I'm grateful to Todd Clear, Bud Brown, Kitty Calavita, Randy Shelden, Shadd Maruna, and Jodi Lane for reading early drafts of the book and giving helpful suggestions for improvement. And to Val Jenness, Gil Geis, Bill Maurer, Susan Will, Joan Petersilia, and Henry Pontell for their useful input before the actual writing really began.

My thanks to the following reviewers for their helpful comments: Susan Pease, Central Connecticut State University; Theodore Sasson, Middlebury College; Kevin Early, Oakland University; Tara Gray, New Mexico State University; Steven Atchley, Delaware Technical and Community College; Barbara Owen, Fresno State University; Jim Austin, George Washington University; and Gil Geis, University of California, Irvine.

I want to express my gratitude to others, whether I know you or not, who have been to prison and are now embarking on an academic trail. A few to whom I am especially grateful include John Irwin, Alan Mobley, Susan Dearing, and Stephen Richards.

Without the fellas, none of this would have been possible. I extend my gratitude to each one of you and hope the future roads we travel are smoother than those we passed before. I would also like to thank all the convicts, former and current, I have been fortunate enough to cross paths with along the way. I am grateful for our continuing relationships. To a large degree, it is "those places" we have been, or still find ourselves in, that give me the energy to do what I'm doing today.

I want to thank Sabra Horne for her ongoing efforts and support in getting this book into production. Much more than an editor, she has become someone I consider to be a genuine friend. As have others from the various worlds I come from, she has been instrumental in helping me learn how to accomplish my goals. I also extend my deepest appreciation to Robin Gold, who copyedited the book, and Kim Fowler at St. Louis University for helping me with the final stages of getting the bibliography in order.

Finally, I'd like to say a humble thanks to my wife Debbie for living with me all these years and for accepting me just the way I am. I hope the day will come that I'll be able to do the same for you.

Foreword

John Irwin

Chuck Terry is a member of an important new community of "ex-convict criminologists." He is an authentic member. He went the full route—thuggery, addiction, and plenty of prison time. Then he got an education. Now he combines his experiences and his academic skills and gives us a close examination of the difficult journeys into and away from addiction. The "fellas" are a group of recovering addicts he met on his own journey out of addiction.

Terry and the rest of the ex-convict criminologists (of whom I am one) are able to get at this type of phenomena—that is, the social worlds of criminals and prisoners—better than almost everyone else. It starts off with our ability to "speak the language," and then to pull close to our research subjects and enter into their meaning worlds. Terry does this with precision and depth and gives us a close, valuable description and analysis of the important transitions these fellas made in their lives as addicts.

He starts by looking at the surrounding society's construction of the images of the drug user and the impact this has on drug users' views of themselves. Then he ushers us through the significant phases of the addicts' lives.

The fellas start from different places—as "regs," "wannabes," and "drifters." But then addiction gets them and they go through incarceration—perhaps several times—which processes them into "ex-convict dopefiends." The group he examines had arrived at a significant juncture and decided to change. Terry examines this turning point and the process of redefinition and reintegration. In all of these different phases, he supplies us with solid, phenomenological material. So, in basic human terms, we understand the transitions. And that is the power of this type of study. Read it with an expectation of coming closer to the experiences of these demi-world denizens.

1

Introduction

One day in March of 1984, I was transported from an Oregon county jail to court for sentencing. During the bus ride, I looked through the steel meshed windows at the outside world and wondered about my future. After arriving, I was escorted into a holding cell, the chains that bound my hands and feet were undone, and I waited to appear before the judge.

When my turn finally came, I noticed that the courtroom was almost empty. Besides myself, the only people present were the judge, the district attorney, my public defender, the court reporter, and a bailiff. Once my name and case were announced, the judge asked the district attorney if he would like to say anything before sentencing:

> Yes, your honor. It is the position of the people that this man is a chronic drug addict, a career criminal, and a menacing threat to society. He has already been to prison and has proven that he is beyond rehabilitation. Therefore, we ask the court to sentence him to the maximum term prescribed by law.

Next, the public defender spoke on my behalf:

> Your honor, my client has a well-documented history of heroin addiction, which is at the root of these charges and his criminal history. Given that he has already been to prison, it seems to me that the court has only two choices in this matter. One would be to give him a suspended sentence and send him to a long-term, live-in drug program where he might really

get a chance at rehabilitation—a place where he might learn about himself, his addiction and what he might do to live a drug free life and become a productive member of society. The only other feasible alternative is obviously prison.

The words spoken by the district attorney and the public defender did not surprise me. I felt anger and hostility toward the "representative of the people" and appreciation for my lawyer. Now it was time for the judge to make his decision:

> Mr. Terry, you come up here from California doing burglaries and shootin' heroin in my county. Then you come into my courtroom asking for a drug program when personally I think if I let you out you'd commence to doin' more burglaries and shootin' more heroin in my county. I sentence you to twenty years in the state penitentiary and highly recommend you do ten years before becoming eligible for parole. Personally, I think you belong penned up for life and I hope you never get out. Bailiff, get this man outta my courtroom.

At the time, the judge's words and their implications were devastating. Now, years later, I can look back at the courtroom morality play with educated eyes and realize that the way I was viewed by the judge, the district attorney, the public defender, and myself had everything to do with the then-current cultural conceptions of heroin addicts. The district attorney portrayed me as being a dangerous criminal in need of a severe sentence. The public defender saw me as a sick individual in need of treatment. The judge saw me as a disgusting, evil person who was beyond any hope of rehabilitation—as if I were an inherently flawed individual. The image I had of myself at that moment reflected, in part, how I was being defined by the courtroom members. A few words now come to mind: angry, desperate, scared, helpless, hopeless, and beat up.

That day I got sentenced was a low point in my life. Though I didn't know it then, I would be spending the next six and a half years inside the Oregon State prison. My parole date was October 5, 1990. Since then I have been married, involved in 12-step programs, school, and a variety of relationships that would have, at one time, seemed impossible. Today I work as an assistant professor at St. Louis University. How I see myself and how others see me today is dramatically different than it was 5, 10, or 15 years ago.

A question that often baffles me is, How did I get to where I am today? At times, it seems that I am living in a different world. In many ways, this is true. In retrospect, it seems that my ever-changing self-concept and subsequent behavior have been affected by how I have interacted with and interpreted the sociohistorical circumstances, conditions, events, and people in my life—all of which are always changing as well. Addressing this issue as it relates to a group of men who, like me, are living relatively normal lives after spending years as heroin addicts and as convicts is what this book is all about.

THE INTERSECTION OF ADDICTION
AND PRISONIZATION

Before my last "reentry" into society in 1990, I considered a few things about myself that I knew would hinder my chances of "doing good"[1] on the outside. First, I realized I was an addict and would have to somehow overcome the negative effects of heroin addiction that had haunted me since I was 18 years old. Having been to prison three times before, always for drug-related crimes, I knew that every effort I made in the past to stay clean eventually failed. However hard I tried not to, I reverted to using heroin. And, because of the desperate things I did to get the drug, I was inevitably propelled into a collision course with agents of the law and a return trip to custody. Second, I realized I had become overly acculturated into the prison environment, or *prisonized,* which is the effect of a process long ago identified as the "taking on in greater or lesser degree . . . the folkways, mores, customs, and general culture of the penitentiary" (Clemmer, 1940, 299). My perspective had become a reflection of the overregulated, upside-down, violence-prone, hypermasculine, and extraordinarily routinized lifestyle common to such institutions. Much of what I believed, including my conceptions of self, others, good versus bad, and right versus wrong, mirrored the norms and values of that peculiar setting. In short, I recognized that to stay out of prison, I would have to struggle with the effects of both addiction *and* prisonization.

Like many of us who reached early adulthood in the late1960s, I experimented with a variety of drugs. Unlike most, however, who never had any serious, lasting problems with drugs, I tried heroin and instantly fell in love. After feeling its powerful effects, I remember thinking, "I can't believe I've been wasting my life doing anything other than shooting this stuff!" Before long, I was hanging around with other addicts, getting arrested, and spending time behind bars. A few times, I did what I thought of as good after being released. Once, I managed to stay off heroin by participating in a methadone maintenance program for 18 months.[2] After finding a job, getting married, and discharging my parole, I decided it was time to leave the program. Unfortunately, methadone is extremely addicting, and the detox process was more than I could handle. Before it was over, I was regularly using heroin again. Shortly thereafter, I returned to prison. On another occasion, I found myself in a situation where I had access to enough money to support my habit without hustling on the street or stealing. During that period, I worked at a regular job, ate well, slept well, and lived what had the appearance of a so-called normal life. When the money (which came from a girlfriend stealing from a store where she worked) ran out, however, I fell back into my old behavioral patterns and soon was arrested again.

---

[1] "Doing good" is a phrase used by prisoners in reference to being successful in the outside world. For a deeper understanding of the term, see Irwin, 1970, 131–148.

[2] Methadone, a synthetic opiate legally administered by public officials, is also used by medical doctors for opiate detoxification and pain management.

Before that particular arrest, which eventually led to my encounter with the judge in the Oregon courtroom, I made phone calls to various hospitals or "recovery" centers asking for help because I was hopelessly addicted and just couldn't stop using. I was tired of the desperation and hopelessness I was living with; the stealing, the hiding, the pain, the remorse, and the sure knowledge that sooner or later I was going back to prison. When someone on the other line answered, I'd say, "Hi. I need help. I'm a heroin addict who has already been to prison twice. I'm hooked like a dog. I'm doing felonies everyday to support my habit, *and can't stop!*" In response to this plea came the inevitable question, "Do you have insurance?" "No," I'd answer as my heart sunk. "I'm sorry, but if you don't have insurance," they'd say, "the cost is five hundred dollars a day." Working through my feelings after being rejected, I'd angrily blurt something into the phone like, "Are you serious? For five hundred a day I can use!" Since that time I've learned a great deal about medical facilities that treat addiction across the country. Though they help many, they are also businesses that exist to make a profit. For the most part, people with money go to places like the Betty Ford Clinic and the poor go to prison, which is exactly where I was headed not long after making those phone calls.

As it has for countless others, the love, attraction, or "pull" of heroin ran very deep for me. And, as I sat in my cell contemplating being released again, I knew that overcoming its powerful lure would be necessary if I were to actually have any chance of staying out. In the past, family and friends often asked me how I could live the way I did so I could use the drug. How could I stand the prison time, sickness, suffering, and shame that was an inherent part of the lifestyle? Today, because I keep little of my past a secret, I have students who ask the same thing. As a response, when time permits, I provide a synopsis of my personal history because only by being able to at least glimpse the entire story can such questions be even partially answered and understood. At other times I merely say, "It's hard to live in hell when you get a taste of heaven."

Another method I use to explain this attraction to people who don't understand addiction, especially those who believe that the habitual use of narcotics is a choice, is to tell a hypothetical story that involves the potential for sex (which most of us *can* understand) in prison. Sex with women in male prisons is, of course, very rare. For me it was always nonexistent and something I missed *a lot*. Now, imagine me sitting in my cell on a day when, like the overwhelming majority of days I spent there, I had no heroin, then the warden coming to me with an option. Because I haven't caused him any problems for six months, I can choose one of two prizes he will make available: I can either leave immediately to embark on a journey with 25 beautiful, female, heterosexual convicts (who have all been isolated from men for years) on a Caribbean cruise with all the luxuries that come with such a trip for six months. Or, I can inject the heroin he pulls out of his pocket right there on the spot. For me, and I would speculate for people who were (or are) addicts like me, there would be no real choice. It wouldn't have mattered if I'd been locked up 10 weeks or 10 years. Moreover, it wouldn't matter if I were physically addicted or not. Without hesitating, I would have chosen the drug.

As well as deal with my addiction-related demons, I knew I would be confronted with the effects of prisonization when I got released. I realized that though I had learned to do quite well while I was locked up, I would basically be a social cripple on the outside. On the inside, the choices I made each day were minimal. I could go to work, take a shower, or go to the yard—or not. Whether the main course was called Salisbury steak, meatloaf, or Swedish meatballs, I knew it was all made from the same mystery meat and I could eat it—or not. As unnatural as it was, I knew I had become dependent on the state to feed, clothe, and house me. Further, my familiarity with the environment brought with it a sense of comfort. I knew what to expect, how to act, who to trust or not trust and that except for the faces of the guards and prisoners, almost nothing ever changed. Finally, I was associated with people who, highly prisonized themselves, would be categorized at the top of the prisoner social hierarchy. Often called "regulars" (Irwin, 1970), these associations helped me do relatively easy time and to be seen with respect by others and myself. I knew that once I was released all this would be gone instantly. Instead, I would feel fear, anxiety, and alienation.

As will be discussed in Chapter 3, many of these regulars had been raised in poor, working-class environments where incidents of violence, drug addiction, and incarceration were a normal and expected way of life. Not only did they typically begin getting arrested and sentenced to various types of juvenile "correctional" facilities when they were 10 or 12 years old, but it was not unusual for their mothers, uncles, cousins, and brothers to be locked up as well. Adjusting to imprisonment for them was easier than it was for people like me who grew up in gentler surroundings.

Those of us who were brought up in more middle class-oriented neighborhoods can be seen as having "drifted" between "criminal" and conventional actions (Matza, 1964) because of our use of illegal drugs. We typically maintained stakes in the mainstream culture, yet dabbled in criminality that was associated with addiction. Compared to regulars, we entered prison as outsiders. Fearful of what to expect, and initially feeling extremely out of place, we tended to step back, watch what was going on, and learn the accepted ways of interacting with others.[3] Over time, many of us became comfortable. To varying degrees, we became prisonized.

Regardless of whether somebody might be classified as a regular or a drifter, the more time we do, the more likely it is we will become prisonized. And the more prisonized we become, the less likely it is we will do good after being released. Add to this a history of chronic drug addiction, and the chances of making a successful transition to the outside world are lessened even more. The tragic story of a woman I recently met illustrates how damaging the effects of

---

[3] For an excellent study about how first time prisoners manage their identities, see Jones and Schmid, 2000.

both addiction and prisonization can be on individuals who are trying to survive after the doors of confinement are opened.

Marisol

Marisol was someone I recently met during a trip I made to California. She and another woman, who I quickly learned were on a pass from a year-long, residential drug program, happened to be making a few bucks cleaning a friend's house when I stopped by for a visit. Marisol and I hit it off right away. The connection we made was sparked by our similar backgrounds. She too had spent many years using heroin and doing time in prison. What made us different was that I had been clean and off parole for many years. She had been clean for less than 30 days and out of prison for only 2 months. As soon as we started talking, I could tell she was struggling to make sense of her world. She told me she had recently been attending 12-step meetings (which indicated she was making an effort to change). But I also sensed that what she found in those meetings, or in the program where she lived, had little meaning for her. It wasn't until she gave me a quick overview of her history, however, that I understood the depths of her suffering.

Marisol told me she was born addicted. Both her parents had been heroin addicts. By the age of 9 or 10, she was taking heroin to guards at a nearby prison who, for a price, would pass it on to her convict father who was an almost permanent resident of the facility. During her early teenage years, she became addicted herself. Before long, she was doing time in juvenile detention facilities. She appeared to be in her mid-30s when we met. By then, she had spent the greater portion of her adulthood in California prisons.

Using the language of a seasoned convict, she told me how alienated she felt out here in the free world. She told me that the reason she was in a live-in program was because her parole officer said it was either that or be returned to custody for having given positive urinalysis tests for heroin. Not surprisingly (because of her prisonized outlook), she complained about all the "bullshit rules" she had to contend with at the program and how she couldn't stand most of the women there because they were all heartless snitches (they were scared and informed on one another to please figures of authority at the house). She said she liked the 12-step meetings a little, but really couldn't relate to most of the people there. Finally, in what seemed to be a desperate plea for help, she told me she didn't know what she was even doing "out here." With gut-wrenching honesty she talked about how her life, her friends, and her world were in the prison she left behind. That was where she fit. That was where her friends were. That was where things had meaning that she could understand.

Listening to her, as I have to many other prison-oriented addicts who were trying to turn their lives around after being paroled, was not easy because I understood her situation so well. I knew how unlikely it was that the course of her life would ever really take a different direction. Still, I did what I could to inspire her by mentioning stories about a few people, including myself, who have walked a path similar to her own and are doing good in the world today. That we, as hard as it has been, have managed to both stay clean *and* stay out. I did my best to explain how she was involved in a process where doing good meant making a successful transition from the world of the addict and convict to the world of living without heroin as a free person on the outside. One of the beautiful things about 12-step programs, I told her, was that they were places where she could make meaningful connections with people like herself—people who have been where she's been, done the things she's done, and are now doing good. If she could develop relationships with just a few such people, I suggested, and ask for their help and follow some of their advice, she too might learn about and experience a better way of living.

I saw Marisol a few times at 12-step meetings before leaving California. We always hugged each other and she always had a smile on her face. Yet I felt the image she was projecting, for the most part, was only a mask. What I didn't know was the direction her immediate future would take. About a week after my return to the Midwest, I received a phone call informing me she had died of an overdose. Although I was hurt by the news, I was not really too surprised. I could tell when we met that she didn't have much of a chance. The sad truth is I've known too many addict/convicts who have died prematurely. Her death seems like such a tragic waste of life. Affected by forces beyond her control, she had become addicted and severely prisonized. The effects of these crippling processes, as they have been for many others, were too much for her to overcome.

EARLY ORIGINS OF THIS STUDY

My motivation to do this research was related to the interest I had in learning more about the circumstances that helped me and other heroin addicts who had been to prison eventually get clean and stay out of prison. I was also influenced by what I learned during my years of formal education that began in prison and continued for many years after my release.

During graduate school, I was presented with information about criminology, law, and society. The basic curriculum focused on classes about theory, statistics, research methods, legal reasoning, and so on. As a teaching assistant, I worked with professors who taught corrections, juvenile delinquency, the law and inequality, deviance, and criminal justice and court procedures. I attended national conferences where "experts" met to present their latest research findings. The content of their material was typically associated with things like the structural covariates of domestic violence, the impact of habitual offender laws on crime, and various relationships within the criminal justice system.

Being exposed to this information was an experience in itself. It often felt strange to be sitting in a classroom listening to a professor talk about issues related to prison and notice that little, if anything, was mentioned about the real lives of prisoners. Similarly, the mostly quantitative research presented in academic journals and conferences had little to do with the actual experiences of any "criminals" I had known. Consequently, I was left with the impression that the creators of this information knew little about the social worlds of the people they were studying.

It was not surprising, therefore, to learn that little effort had been made to understand the subjective experiences of those defined as criminals and prisoners. Except for a multitude of inquiries using statistics as the basis of explanation, and a few qualitative studies done about addicts or prisoners, I discovered there had been little ethnographic work done regarding the lives of people who had successfully overcome the effects of both heroin addiction *and* prisonization. For example, Biernacki (1986) looked at how self-concepts were central to the change that took place among a group of addicts who quit using heroin without treatment. However, not everyone in his sample had to battle the effects of spending years behind bars.

So, while considering a topic for my dissertation I asked myself, "What can I, with my background, contribute to this field?" The answer seemed simple, straightforward, and potentially worthwhile. I can tell about what I know—drug addiction, prisonization, recovery,[4] and reintegration. The social circumstances I found myself in were ideal for accomplishing such a task. My personal associations with members of 12-step programs, several of whom were involved in the process I was interested in studying, made it relatively easy to locate enough people to make the project possible.

IDENTITY TRANSFORMATION
AS A MEANS OF OVERCOMING
ADDICTION AND PRISONIZATION

It is my belief that to turn our lives around, people with backgrounds like Marisol and me have to undergo the difficult task of learning to see ourselves differently. This is why I chose to make identity transformation the focus of this book. To examine this process, I decided to interview a sample of male, ex-heroin addicts who had all been to prison and look at how their self-concepts changed over time. To accomplish this, I attempted to discover the situations, turning points and significant others that helped alter the meanings of things in their lives and the actions they have taken as a result of these changed meanings. In short, I wanted to better understand the processes that helped them "get clean" and leave behind lifestyles centered around drug addiction, criminality, and imprisonment.

---

[4] "Recovery is a process in which the physical, psychological, emotional, and social damage caused by addiction is being healed" (Landry, 1994, 159). It is also used by people in 12-step programs who see themselves as "recovering" from the "disease" of alcoholism or addiction (Conrad and Schneider, 1992, 73–109; Denzin, 1987).

My interviews and interactions with the men took place just before the new millennium, and in many ways, the things I heard were shaped by historical context. Like my own experience in front of the Oregon judge, their lives were influenced by the anti-drug sentiments of the1980s. Of importance is the idea that each of the courtroom views was peculiar to when and where they occurred. In a different time and place, say 20, 40, or 90 years earlier, the beliefs of everyone involved would have been different and a reflection of the perspectives of the period. Imprisoning addicts has not always been an accepted social policy.

I begin by telling part of the story about the social history of drugs in the United States, with an emphasis on how the cultural images of users have continually shifted over the past 150 years. I illustrate how certain groups of addicts came to be demonized in the 19th century and the way these negative characterizations were used to criminalize certain forms of drug use. I hope that this brief familiarization with history will provide a better understanding of how we think about and treat addicts today.

The bulk of the story, however, is about the lives of the men I was fortunate enough to interview whom I collectively call the "fellas." Most were actively involved with the 12-step programs of either Alcoholics Anonymous (AA) or Narcotics Anonymous (NA) at the time of the interviews. As you will see, many of the changes they experienced were influenced by the relationships they developed as members of these programs. What many of them gained by participating in AA or NA was a guide to living that, in turn, helped them construct more positive self-evaluations.

Perhaps the greatest barrier people like the fellas have to face, and one that can be mitigated with strong social support (as can be found in family relationships or 12-step programs) is their deeply held belief that they are inferior human beings. Overcoming a sense of being an outright alien while interacting in everyday, mainstream activities is something many of them have struggled with for years. As I will show in greater detail in the pages to come, the effects of such negative self-concepts can be so crippling that doing ordinary things like buying groceries in a store or asking somebody for a job can be overwhelming.

Explaining the potential depth of this alienation is difficult. Recently, I made an effort to get an ex-convict support group going because I believe newly released prisoners can benefit tremendously by interacting with people who have successfully made the transition from living in prison to the outside world. It's not that we can't get help from others. We can. But who else can *really* understand us? Who else can we *really* relate to in any meaningful way, especially when we first get out? So, one day I met these two guys at a local McDonald's restaurant. James, who had been out nearly two years, was working, had a girlfriend, and was generally doing good. In contrast, Roy had been out for about six months, was unemployed, and obviously struggling. As we entered, James said he wasn't hungry. After quickly purchasing a cup of coffee, he left to find a table leaving Roy and me at the counter looking at the menu on the wall. After I ordered a quarter pounder and a cup of coffee, I told Roy to go ahead and get whatever he wanted—this one was on me. At that moment, he turned his head toward me and whispered in my ear, "I'll just get whatever you're getting. Doing this kind of thing is still too intimidating to me. And I know you understand." Yes, but I had also forgotten because I'd been out so long. I had forgotten about the brightness of the colors in supermarket aisles or on "Happy Meal" signs, about how intimidating it could be to say anything at all to a female because I hadn't done so for such a long time. I had forgotten about how crippling it can be to feel so afraid of being seen as an outsider that you become paralyzed and unable to act, even while doing something as simple as ordering food at McDonald's.

For the fortunate among us, this sense of alienation decreases over time as the way we see ourselves changes. Pelon, one of the fellas who will be introduced in more detail in Chapter 3, addressed this issue in a roundabout way during our interview. He was telling me how, even after being clean and out for many years, receiving a compliment from someone can still make him feel uncomfortable. He recalled a time when the head of the academic department where he was attending graduate school told him, "You're a very admirable person. You're trustworthy." In response, he thought, "There's something wrong here. These are the kind of words I've never heard before." What was "wrong" were not the words she uttered, but the negative conception he had of himself that contradicted the positive things she was saying. Using an example of another situation that he had experienced just the previous day, he said, "My computer wasn't working right, so I had to go and tell my boss that I had just turned in two files by hand. And as I talked to her I noticed my tattoos and thought, 'Oh man, this lady probably thinks I'm an ex-con and a dopefiend.'" His sense of alienation, however, was short lived. He told me that his feelings of inferiority were not as strong as they had been in the past. Nor do they occur as often or last as long. What happens, he said, is that now he is more aware of both his thoughts and their effects. This awareness, which has grown over time, helps him see himself during uncomfortable situations from a different perspective. This, in turn, brings him relief. On another occasion, for example, he said he felt alienated at a party his wife was giving for a group of teachers. "So, I'm there," he told me, "and I started feeling out of place. But right away I snapped out of it. I said, 'Man, forget that thinking. You're here. Just have a good time. Whatever these people think they're not saying anything so just go along with it.'" When I mentioned that I still feel out of place at times, he said, "Man, it happens. But what's happening is I don't let it stop me anymore. Whereas before I would just not even go somewhere. And if I'm somewhere and it comes up I try and see that it's happening within me." That he experiences alienation less often and is able to go places he would have previously avoided shows how much he has changed.

Though Pelon had been clean for quite awhile, he attributed much of his success at reintegration to the early days of his recovery, which began by attending NA meetings in jail. He said it took him awhile to believe it, but eventually the meetings had a positive effect on the way he thought about himself. "People would come in [to the jail]. I'd hear their stories and start identifying a little more and a little more with what they said. I got to where I was thinking, 'Maybe I can do this. Maybe it's not impossible for me to go out there and get a job and stay clean, feel good about myself, all these things.'" As with many of the fellas, his exposure to the message of hope shared by people from 12-step programs became a means of inspiration and change.

At the outset, it is important to note that this is not an effort to promote 12-step programs, which, when it comes to "curing" people, have a very low batting average. So do psychiatrists, therapists, penitentiaries, county jails, and all sorts of drug programs. Varying definitions of addiction and methodological limitations make it impossible to know how many people are addicts or how many people overcome their addiction-related lifestyles. Yet, it is safe to assume that most people with backgrounds like the fellas will never do as well as the fellas have in their recovery. Yet, it is safe to assume that only a very small proportion of people with backgrounds like the fellas achieve the level of recovery many of them have accomplished. The value of their stories is that they show us what is possible, something that can be improved upon and extended to reach more people, and the strength of the human spirit. Sometimes inspirational, sometimes comical, and at other times tragic, what they reveal is nothing less than a powerful illustration of the human struggle.

THEORETICAL BACKDROP

The research presented here uses a career or life history approach to better understand how individuals see themselves, the effect this perception has on their behavior, and how it changes over time. Life history studies focus on processes of social interaction, how people define situations and turning points in their lives (Ebaugh, 1988; Jacobs, 1969; Lofland, 1966; Rosenbaum, 1981; Strauss, 1969). Further, they concentrate on "career contingencies," which are factors that influence social mobility. "Career contingencies include both the objective facts of social structure and changes in the perspectives, motivations, and desires of the individual" (Becker, 1963, 24). Heroin addicts, for example, might be released from prison because they are granted parole. They go from prison to the free world because they are granted parole. The "outcome" of their time spent in the free world, which is contingent on their being paroled, will be affected by the environments they return to and their perspectives. A life history approach makes it possible to examine these contingencies and the underlying processes that affect the way they are interpreted and experienced:

> Life histories seek to establish the process whereby personal circumstances are interpreted by the person giving the account so as to produce the actions related in the account. Particular attention is given to the temporal sequences of events, the social context in which they occurred, their interpretations by the individual, and how all this led him or her to believe and behave as he or she did. (Ebaugh, 1988, 32)

A basic premise of this study is that the "worlds" that exist for people are made up of "objects" and that these objects are the result of symbolic interaction. From this standpoint, an object is anything that can be referred to, thought about, or indicated, such as something physical (for example, a tree or car), social (a mother or teacher), or abstract (moral ideology or alienation). People actively construct the way they see themselves and their worlds based on the meanings they give to the objects in their lives. These meanings, which are developed during an ongoing process of social interaction, determine how an object is seen, acted upon, talked about and so forth (Blumer, 1969, 10–11).

The nature of any object will always depend entirely on what it means to a specific individual or group. Understanding these meanings opens windows into worlds and helps explain behavior. Objects may mean different things to different people: a gram of black tar heroin will likely be something very different for an addict suffering from withdrawals than it will be for a narcotics officer, a drug program supervisor, or the husband of a woman who recently died from an overdose; a union strike can be a very different event in the eyes of workers compared with their employers; the Civil Rights movement of the 1960s was seen as a needed push for social change by some and a threat to the status quo by others. Understanding how the "fellas" defined the objects in their lives and how these meanings changed helps explain the effects of the worlds from which they came, and how their self-concepts and behavior evolved over time.

The *self*, from the perspective of a symbolic interactionist, is an object, like all other things. Over the life course, the self evolves as new circumstances, situations, and associations with others come into play. People act according to their interpretations of these events, the way they see themselves, and the way they think others will react toward them. "A social self of this sort might be called the reflected or looking-glass self" (Cooley, 1996, 63).

Proponents of labeling theory (Becker, 1963; Lemert, 1996; Tannenbaum, 1938), an offshoot of symbolic interaction, suggest that deviant self-concepts are formed as a result of individuals being defined as deviant. The process takes place when people use definitions given to them by others to evaluate themselves. When, over time, those definitions become central to their self-concepts, the process is complete. By being defined as a criminal for using illegal drugs, for example, it is possible that an individual will come to see himself as a criminal. Self-concepts, then, can be influenced by the impressions of others in one's social world and by societal reaction.

It is easy to see how this might happen. Take, for example, a 13-year-old boy who gets caught with marijuana at school. He is condemned by school administrators and, perhaps, suspended for a period of time. His parents punish him and express shame for his behavior. He is called ignorant, stupid, out of control, and told that if he doesn't change he will turn into a worthless drug addict. Then he is caught again, this time with marijuana and alcohol. Again, he is disciplined and stigmatized. Only this time it's worse. The negative manner in which he is being evaluated has a powerful effect. Because he believes it, it becomes real for him. In time, he begins to see himself and act in a manner consistent with the label. Before long, he is doing time in juvenile detention facilities. When he reaches adulthood, he finds himself in prison.

A true story provides another illustration. One day after giving a lecture about parts of my own life experiences to a large university class, a young woman approached me outside the classroom. After telling me she liked my talk, she informed me that she also used to have a drug problem. She said that even though she was an "A" student, she used methamphetamine (speed), marijuana, and alcohol almost everyday from the eighth through the twelfth grade. By the time she left high school, she began noticing many of the people she got high with were heading down a path she did not want to share, so she quit. I asked her if she ever thought of herself as an addict during all those years of drug use. She told me no. When I asked her why, she said, "Probably because I never got caught." Having never been caught, disciplined, and labeled as an addict, she never saw herself as one. This, in turn, likely helped her venture onward toward newer, brighter horizons.

Critics of labeling theory point out that it does nothing to explain the onset of deviant behavior.[5] Yet its relevance here has to do with the stigma (Goffman, 1963) associated with being seen as a criminal and a heroin addict. To varying degrees, the societal reaction to heroin use and criminality experienced by addicts who go to prison has an influence over their lives, self-concepts, and actions.

The ideas presented in this book, many of which were greatly influenced by the teachings of Tamotsu Shibutani, a respected sociologist and friend, are based on the assumption that self-concepts and behavior are closely linked. Theoretically, change in one affects change in the other. "A self-concept consists of a set of beliefs and presuppositions . . . [about oneself as an object and] is the product of participation in a long succession of social transactions" (Shibutani, 1986, 164). It can be assumed that changing self-concepts are related to one's reference groups and interpretations of situations and events throughout the life course.

The idea of a reference group is useful in explaining changing self-concepts and behavior. As members of modern society, we are exposed to many perspectives, all of which are related to beliefs and value systems of people from diverse social worlds. Consider, for instance, academia, religious sects, adolescence, business, or homelessness. Within each are organized ways of thinking, seeing, and acting, characterized by different expectations and unique styles of communication. Yet, we identify more with some than others. Perhaps the greatest degree of solidarity within these worlds can be found in those that do not fall within mainstream norms. Examples might include social elites, newly arrived immigrants, or heroin addicts who have been to prison. A reference group is that group whose outlook is used as a frame of reference for making judgements and decisions (Shibutani, 1972). The view of the reference group we relate to the most acts as a lens through which we see the world.

---

[5] Interactionists would argue that, because of the complexity of social life, attempts to nail down specific "causes" of deviance are impractical.

Self-concepts can change as one has new experiences. Such revisions generally occur when individuals become involved with new groups or begin participating in different activities (Shibutani, 1986). For example, one might begin attending a new school or obtain employment in a completely different field. Learning from the doctor about an inoperable cancer, unexpectedly inheriting a large sum of money, moving from southern California to Calcutta, India, or being sentenced to death might also affect one's self-evaluation.

Much of what the fellas told me about seeing themselves differently and the changing direction of their lives had to do with them developing new reference groups. "All forms of social mobility . . . may be regarded essentially as displacements of reference groups, for they involve a loss of responsiveness to the demands of one social world and the adoption of the perspective of another" (Shibutani, 1972, 24). Addicts and ex-convicts who are trying to do good will benefit by developing new relationships and self-concepts that either exclude or depreciate their old values. At the same time, they need to be accepted within new social worlds and not condemned for past actions (Biernacki, 1986; Maruna, 2001).

CHARACTERISTICS OF THE FELLAS[6]

All of the fellas had lived as heroin addicts and prisoners, so it is likely that their general perspectives remained, to some degree, a reflection of the reference groups that are central to these two marginalized groups. During the time of data collection, they had been or currently were involved in drug treatment, 12-step programs, or both. Instead of associating with prisoners and active heroin addicts, they were interacting with others (often ex-prisoners or clean addicts) who provided them with a new way of looking at the world. "As one's reference group changes, the demands and obligations one feels also change" (Shibutani, 1986, 115). Participation in these programs offers a way for a labeled deviant to become delabeled as a stigmatized person and relabeled as a former and repentant deviant (Trice and Roman, 1978).

The sample consisted of 20 men. Six were Chicanos, 11 were white, 2 were black, and 1 was Mexican.[7] All except 3 had life histories that have taken place, for the most part, in the southern California area (one came from New York, two from Oregon). Their ages ranged from 42 to 61 (mean age = 48). The time they spent incarcerated ranged from 3 to 27 years (mean time spent inside = 10.8 years). The amount of time they had been living clean, drug-free lives varied considerably from a minimum of 30 days to 16 years (mean clean time = 5.4 years).

---

[6] For information about how I located the fellas, the interview process, and what was done to protect them, see the Appendix.

[7] Chicanos, who are descendants of Mexicans, are born in the United States. In southern California, they often see themselves differently than native-born Mexicans do. The low number of African Americans reflected the very small black community found in the area where the study was done.

No effort was made to validate this basic demographic information. The rapport I had with these men left me little doubt as to their honesty. Besides, what I was looking for would not have been affected if some of them stretched the truth about, for example, how much prison time they had done or their length of clean time. How they characterized themselves within their stories about the social worlds of prison, heroin addiction, and recovery would have been difficult to fabricate, and that is what I was after.

THE FELLAS IN CONTEXT
AND THE VALUE OF THEIR STORY

This study is particularly timely because in recent years more and more people are being incarcerated for drug law violations. In fact, escalating numbers of prison commitments for drug offenses greatly explain the skyrocketing rates of imprisonment that have plagued the United States during the past 20 years (Austin and Irwin, 2001; Baum, 1996; Mauer, 1999). The number of people behind bars for drugs today is about the same as the total number locked up for *all crimes* in 1980. Further, the United States has about 100,000 more people in prison for drug charges than the European Union has *for all offenses* (Schiraldi et al., 2000). Although it is true that, for some, the idea of being sent to prison can deter behavior, including drug use, I would argue that the effects of this massive prison build up do far more damage than good. From my standpoint, this trend is nothing less than a wide-scale prescription for separating families and tearing apart inner city neighborhoods that are most affected by these policies (Clear et al., 2001; Hagan and Coleman, 2001), *and generating prisonization.*

With so many people going *to* prison, more are getting *out* than ever before. Research on prisoner reentry to the community, which is currently a hotly debated topic in the criminal justice field, provides alarming statistics that deserve attention. For example, a report from the Urban Institute tells us that each year roughly 600,000 people are being released from state and federal prisons. Two thirds of these are expected to be rearrested within three years (Travis et al., 2001). Findings from the California State Legislative Analyst's Office claim that 85 percent of released prisoners in that state have drug and alcohol problems, 70 to 80 percent remain unemployed a year after their release, 50 percent are illiterate, and 10 percent are homeless. The numbers are not much different across the country. The Bureau of Justice Statistics reports that nationwide, 82 percent of people on parole who are returned to prison abuse drugs and alcohol, 40 percent are unemployed, roughly 75 percent have not completed high school, and 19 percent are homeless (Butterfield, 2000). These numbers are due, in part, to the get-tough-on-crime, punitive-natured criminal justice policies that have supplanted the rehabilitative model over the past few decades—a matter that will be discussed in the next chapter.

The focus on prisoner reentry, as important as it is, should not detract us from the bigger problem, which is that too many people are being incarcerated in the first place. Today we are locking up more people (many who could be dealt with less harshly) for longer periods in institutions that have the tendency to hinder rather than enhance the likelihood of successful community integration. From 1978 to 1996, for example, the types of crimes people were imprisoned for in this country increased as follows: violent crimes doubled, nonviolent crimes tripled, and drug crimes increased sevenfold. Based on this data, which was generated by the U.S. Justice Department, researchers concluded that 77 percent of new arrivals to America's prisons during this period were incarcerated for nonviolent crimes (Irwin et al., 1999). These punitive actions have crippling effects on individuals, families, and communities (Clear et al., 2001). In short, we are assisting in the creation of a class of prisonized or "throw away people." As the story of the fellas shows, however, we are wrong to believe that people who make mistakes, *including hard-core, drug-injecting convicts,* are beyond change.

Understanding the struggles the fellas have confronted, and in many cases overcome, is useful because battling the effects of prisonization and heroin addiction can last a lifetime. A recent study did a 33-year follow-up of a group of 581 male heroin addicts who had been interviewed in a California prison-based, rehabilitation facility for addicts in the early1960s. Back then, the group averaged a bit higher than 25 years of age. In the recent update on these men's lives, researchers found that of those who remained alive, more than half were still using the drug. Nearly 14 percent had died by the mid-1970s, and half had died by 1996–1997, mostly from overdoses. Chronic liver disease, cancer, heart disease, and AIDS were other leading causes of death. Overall, the survivors had extensive mental and physical problems. The most promising finding indicated that those who had abstained from heroin for more than five years were less likely to engage in criminal behavior or suffer from health problems (Hser et al., 2001).

Finally, heroin addiction in this country is a huge economic burden. Recent estimates suggest that in 1996 alone it cost $21.9 billion to deal with the effects of this social problem. These numbers were based on data generated from the four broad areas of medical care, lost productivity in the workplace, crime, and social welfare (Mark et al., 2001). Of course, these are dollars that all of us are called upon to pay.

To place the fellas' story within a historical context, Chapter 2 provides a brief overview of how the self-concepts and actions of people addicted to opiates (and other illegal drugs) have been affected by the social construction of addiction as first deviant, then criminal. Using stories from newspapers, magazines, books and television, I examine how addicts have been characterized in the popular culture from the mid-19th century until modern times. Further, I illustrate that how addicts see themselves is related to how they are viewed by others. Using pseudonyms to ensure their anonymity, Chapter 3 introduces the fellas. I also address the differences found regarding their "ways into" lifestyles centered around addiction that include where they came from, what

was going on in their lives when they began using drugs, and their early experiences of incarceration. Chapter 4 provides a representation of the ways they
adapted to the changing social world of the prison and how their self-concepts
evolved to reflect various degrees of prisonization. Chapter 5 outlines some of
their long-term patterns of behavior and discusses how they developed negative self-evaluations that were influenced by the conditions and situations of
their lives. Much of their motivation to change stemmed from these negative
self-evaluations and a desperate need to find another way to live. In Chapter
6, I talk about how the men became involved in drug treatment and 12-step
programs, the relationships they subsequently cultivated, and the actions they
took that helped them develop more positive self-evaluations and new perspectives. Chapter 7 provides some final thoughts as well as an update on how
the fellas were doing three years after the initial interviews.

2

What Came Before and the Construction of Addict Images

One of my earliest impressions of heroin addicts was how different they seemed to be from other people I had known. They seemed to unquestioningly accept aspects of their lives that would likely make so-called "normal" people cringe. To support their habits, many of the women worked as prostitutes, shoplifted from stores, or did the bidding of males who sold the drug to make ends meet. The men, on the other hand, appeared to play a variety of roles that centered around some form of criminal activity. They sold dope, did armed robberies, forgeries, burglaries, or shoplifted. For many of them, spending time behind bars was as much a part of life as waking up in the morning. I remember feeling that something was terribly wrong when I would hear them loudly vomiting in the county jail because they were suffering from withdrawals. And that sense of wrongness becoming stronger when I began doing the same thing myself. In the midst of it all I often wondered, why is it we have to live like this? Why is it that people think of us and treat us like scum?

It wasn't until years later that I started learning about the history that preceded me—a history that, when understood, helps explain why incarcerating addicts is so prevalent and accepted today. It also illustrates that the reason many of us unquestionably accept the conditions of our lives is because we see ourselves as we have been portrayed by others.

SELF-CONCEPTS AND SELF-IMAGES

Most of us have a general idea of who we are, an identity or self-concept; ways we describe and think of ourselves (Harre, 1998; Shibutani, 1991). So, if asked, a woman might define herself as, among other things, married or good natured or hard working or an ex-convict or as a mother of four with a strong belief in God. In contrast to self-concepts, which are often never considered,[1] are self-images, which have to do with how we see ourselves in specific situations. The same woman might see herself differently at her parole board hearing than she would at her wedding. Self-images are related to self-consciousness and usually come about during periods of strain, opposition, or struggle (Shibutani, 1991). During such moments negative attitudes about addicts can have profound effects.

Negative and demonizing public attitudes about drug use affect the self-concepts and behaviors of people who have been or are addicted to opiates. This is not the same as saying ideas about drug use cause individuals to see themselves or act in certain ways. Throughout history, there have been people who resisted the implications of popular stereotypes. However, the cultural meanings of opiates, especially heroin, do influence lives. "What a person becomes, including how he behaves, will depend in large measure on the way he has been and continues to be assessed and defined by others" (Quinney, 1970, 244).

Heroin addicts today are treated as both deviant and criminal. But it has not always been this way. As this chapter illustrates, how others see them, including representatives of the law, has to do with sets of ideas and images that coexist within a continuously evolving political context. This becomes evident as we notice the contradictory manner in which perceptions and ways of dealing with them are different within either a given historical period, or over time. These images, which help create stereotypes, are diffused into the popular culture and become the basis for how people see those defined as criminal (Quinney, 1970).

NINETEENTH-CENTURY ADDICTS
IN THE UNITED STATES

Historically, poor images of heroin users in the United States can be traced to Chinese immigrants who came to California to work as laborers in the mid-19th century and introduced the smoking of opium to America. Until roughly 1870, few whites participated in this activity. They were hostile to the different group and found Chinese customs to be strange. Moreover, whites feared that cheap "coolie" labor would cause them to lose their jobs (Sandmeyer, 1939).

---

[1] Most of us do not spend much, if any, time consciously thinking about how we generally see ourselves. There are exceptions, of course, such as when one undergoes critical self-analysis in a therapeutic setting.

Opium smokers of more than a century past were often characterized as being something less than human. A writer of the period, in his depiction of a New York opium addict, provides an example:

> He stares out upon us with terrible eyes—eyes that dilate with some strange interior light; ferocious yet unaggressive eyes; fixed full upon us and yet absolutely devoid of that unconscious response for which we look in human eyes as distinguishing them from those of brutes. This is the gaze of what is called an "opium devil," one who is supremely possessed by the power of the deadly narcotic on which he has leaned so long. Without opium he cannot live; though human blood runs in his veins, it is little better than poppy juice; he is no longer really a man, but a malignant essence informing a cadaverous human shape. (Lathrop, 1880, 417)

Critics of a hundred years ago identified opium smokers with immorality, filth, and a decadent Chinese culture and filled the popular culture with negative racial images. Warning readers about the spread of this "pestilence," a newspaper writer described the lowly depths to which users could be drawn:

> To gratify his craving for the drug, he must lie on a filthy pallet in a miserable, nasty den . . . side by side with Chinamen and creatures, male and female, to whom, before he acquainted the habit, he would not condescend a nod on the street. (*New York Times,* February 21, 1881, P1[7])

The author warns that the evil activity is responsible for infecting "young men or boys verging on manhood . . . In San Francisco, Virginia City, Portland, Oregon, Salt Lake City, and, in fact, in every town on the coast where there is a Chinaman (*New York Times,* February 21, 1881, P1[7]).

Gamblers, prostitutes, and members of the underworld, already stigmatized because of their behaviors, were not inhibited from crossing racial lines. In addition, rebellious and adventure-seeking young males were attracted into this Chinese social world (Courtwright, 1982). Such individuals were already living outside mainstream society and were not as likely to have self-concepts that would keep them from interacting with the Chinese and experimenting with opium.

Not all users of opiates lived outside the norms of society. Many were people who began opiate use for medical reasons. Morphine, for example, was given to soldiers during the Civil War and many veterans "became morphinists to relieve the pain and suffering following injuries received in the service" (Crothers, 1902, quoted in Terry and Pellens [1928] 1970, 69). After the war these men, many of whom remained addicted for the rest of their lives, either ate opium or used morphine to feed their addiction (Courtwright, 1978, 1982). Unlike the Chinese and white members of the underworld who used the drug for pleasure, however, addicted soldiers were not stigmatized.

Contradictory perceptions of addicts during this period stemmed from medical users being portrayed as sickly victims of the habit while pleasure users were seen as being socially and morally inept. It was one thing to be an upstanding, white businessman who developed the habit for medical reasons, and quite another to be a Chinaman, gambler, or prostitute who enjoyed the use of the narcotic. As Durkheim ([1893] 1964) pointed out long ago, mainstream populations typically stigmatize the behavior of those who live beyond the generally accepted norms of society.

That pleasure users were depicted as immoral, evil, and sick can be seen as a reflection of Protestant religious beliefs that dominated in the late 19th century United States. A major tenet of the Protestant value system had to do with incorporating a strong work ethic. Honesty, hard work, having a close personal relationship with God, and obeying the rules were seen as indicators of moral superiority and a predestined future in heaven (Weber, 1958). Unlike Catholics, who felt that individuals could be forgiven if they repented their sins, Protestants believed that people who did not adhere to their worldview were doomed to rot in hell—that they were sinners by nature and beyond redemption.

Another group of respected individuals who used the drug without condemnation in the 19th century were doctors (Courtwright, 1982; Morgan, 1981; Musto, 1973). Though their use was seen as unfortunate, the cause was associated with situations that did not include pleasure and were, therefore, more acceptable. Doctors, a writer at the turn of the 20th century argued, "begin to use spirits, opium and other drugs for functional and transient disturbances, and later contract serious organic diseases, the early drug-taking having been a contributory cause" (Crothers, 1900, 46).

Unlike the majority of pleasure users who tended to come from the lower ranks of society, medical users most often came from the middle to upper classes. Most of these well-to-do addicts were middle-aged women[2] who began the use of opiates as a remedy to some type of health problem (Courtwright, 1982; Morgan, 1981). A physician of the time explains:

> Opium is to-day a greater curse than alcohol, and justly claims a larger number of helpless victims, which have not come from the ranks of reckless men and fallen women, but the majority of them are to be found among the educated and most honored and useful members of society; and as to sex, we may count out the prostitutes so much given to this vice, and still find females far ahead so far as numbers are concerned. (Hull, 1885, quoted in Morgan, 1974, 39)

Compelling to the patriarchal society was the belief that the problem was the result of an inherent flaw in women. "It is especially those of nervous temperament and excitable natures that are subject to neuralgias and who become easily familiar with morphin" (Jouet, 1883, quoted and translated in Terry and Pellens, [1928] 1970, 98).

More likely, opiates functioned as an alternative to alcohol and a relief for pain. Living amidst what history has labeled the American Temperance Movement, the consumption of alcohol during this time was intensely frowned upon, especially when it was a woman doing the drinking (Gusfield, 1986).

---

[2] For information about the prevalence of women users compared to men during this period, see Terry and Pellens, [1928] 1970, 12–13, 96–97, 469–475.

The intensity of this stigma seemingly increased relative to social position: the higher the status, the greater the stigma. A popular magazine at the beginning of the 20th century reported that the

> Catholic Abstinence Union of America [was calling for] the establishment of women's total abstinence societies because . . . the drinking customs of society to-day foster the use of intoxicants among women—women of the higher grade of society, women of culture, wealth, and influence . . . In so far as women of this class lead society, their evil threatens all. (*Harper's Bazaar,* February 2, 1901, 317)

It is largely a consequence of the larger political and ideological discourse in the late 19th century, then, that women who drank alcohol were stigmatized more severely than men. At the same time, their use of opiates during this period was more socially acceptable than drinking alcohol. Moreover, opium-based medicines were readily available, did not require a doctor's prescription, and could be easily obtained from the local grocery store (Courtwright, 1982). Instead of being seen as immoral or bad, these women were more commonly viewed as unfortunate victims of the opium habit.

Changing Images

The developing cultural perception that users of opiates were victims of a disease and in need of a cure fit the tortured self-concepts of addicts that were surfacing in the confessional literature of the time (e.g., De Quincey, [1821] 1966). From this view, the habitual taking of the drug was "not a vice . . . but a disease . . . requiring . . . proper medical aid and systematic treatment to effect a cure" (*New York Times,* December, 30, 1877). Those who were addicted deserved to be pitied and cured instead of "condemned, censured, and scorned." The drug, which in earlier days had been seen as a cure, became the cause of disease. In particular, it was associated with withdrawal, which has all the markings of a serious illness. One intellectual habituate of the period, whose repeated efforts to quit the habit failed for many years, provided his view of the withdrawal experience:

> A freezing perspiration broke out over the whole body, alternated with flashes of heat. At one moment I felt as if buried deep in Arctic snows; the next as though I lay on a lake of burning lava . . . At length a bilious diarrhea set in, accompanied with vomiting of a dark, bilious matter. Sometimes . . . after vomiting I could lie back in bed and doze for perhaps five minutes. This was the only sleep I had, and the only cessation of my sufferings, night or day, for a week. (Layard, 1874, 703–704)

As these stories spread, the image of an addict was acquiring a sinister shape. By the 1870s and 1880s, the socially prescribed "solution" for "victims" of the habit was seen as being some type of medical cure, one that contemporary "experts" are still seeking.

During this same period, sentiments about the need for laws to control the use of opiates, especially among pleasure users, escalated. The situation in Nevada at the time is telling:

This state has enacted stringent laws against the keeping of opium dens, and has attempted to prohibit smoking [use for pleasure], but the courts have held that the vice does not constitute a crime . . . In all the interior towns every Chinese wash-house, store, and house of prostitution is an opium den, frequented night and day by boys, men, and white prostitutes. The [national] prohibition put upon the importation of opium is a step in the right direction. (*New York Times,* February 21, 1881, P1[7])

As the 19th century came to a close, opiate use had risen to the level of a social problem, and people began considering potential solutions. Much like today, the debate tended to be mostly legal or treatment oriented. Drug use, however, was not yet illegal, and users did not see themselves as criminal simply because they used narcotics. Though addicts who began their habits for pleasurable rather than medicinal purposes were more readily condemned, users were not generally viewed as threatening, fearful, and in need of formal social control. Yet, this impression was in the process of changing.

1900 ONWARD

By the turn of the 20th century, much of the medical community viewed addicts as individuals who suffered from a psychobiological disease, and doctors attempted to develop cures. Many of these "cures" involved the use of medications—some that turned out to be addicting as well. Heroin, which in 1898 was introduced as a cough suppressant and taken orally, is a good example. Originally, heroin came in pill form. When crushed, it could be sniffed, giving the user a quick rush. The drug was cheap, available, and easy to use. It became popular among already addicted people (who used it as a substitute for opium, which was becoming increasingly banned and harder to obtain) and among young, white, city-dwelling males who used it for pleasure (Bailey, 1916; Courtwright, 1982; Morgan, 1981).

Although not entirely without merit, the popular belief held today that heroin was commonly seen as a cure for morphine addiction is debatable. Heroin was quickly identified as being addicting and, thereafter, was not as readily prescribed. Still, for many years, it was easily accessible and its use was less stigmatized. As the availability of opium and morphine dwindled with the advent of legislation, and as the stigma associated with addiction to other narcotics escalated, the use of heroin became more popular (Courtwright, 1982).

Treatment

Doctors were not a prestigious group in the early 20th century, and their position suffered with increased public awareness that their treatment of addicts was seldom successful. Faced with treatment failures, physicians developed a self-serving hypothesis to explain continued drug use. It was not medical failure. Rather, there were two distinct addict types: nonthreatening respectable citizens who were amenable to a cure and "fiends" who were uncontrollable and dangerous (Lichtenstein, 1914; McGuire and Lichtenstein, 1916). By the mid-1920s, the prevailing medical view held that addiction and criminality were related to a psychopathic personality and could be cured with proper treatment.[3] There was either "the "accidental" addict, who [began use] for relief of pain; and the larger group of those who take to narcotics because of nervous instability—because they possess psychopathic personalities" (Sceleth and Kuh, 1924, 682). From this perspective, addicts were seen as "persons who are neurotic or who have some form of twisted personality . . . Such persons are highly susceptible to addiction because narcotics supply them with a form of adjustment of their difficulties" (Kolb, 1925, 312).

Articles published in medical journals of the time reinforced the perspective that addicts were psychopaths, giving the idea heightened credibility. They were typically depicted as being "sick; sick of a definite and demonstrable disease" (Bishop, 1912, quoted in Terry and Pellens, [1928] 1979, 560). A doctor from the period explains:

> The problem of the underlying causes of narcotic addiction lie in the psychology and personality of the individual, and so does the solution to the problem. If you can solve the individual problem which leads to the addiction, you will solve the means by which the individual can be freed from his addiction. (*Literary Digest,* 1920, 28)

Doctors did not agree about the cause and treatment of opiate addiction. Some, who daily dealt with addicts, believed it was a disease that affected all people equally. Treatment should be sought, they argued, but a true cure had not yet been found. Moreover, until a valid cure was developed, addicts should be allowed access to narcotics (Sterne, 1905; Terry, 1920a, 1920b, 1921).

This "pro-maintenance" perspective held that laws attempting to control narcotic use created a black market and pushed many addicts into crime. It urged people to examine the situation in which the addict finds him or herself. If this were done, the perspective held, it would become clear that the actions addicts take are anything but abnormal. They suffer from the inability to stop using narcotics and are stigmatized for their dilemma. While seeking treatment, they are dealt with as outcasts. Usually they fail in their attempts to quit. The pull of the drug is so strong that they are left to participate in secretive, often criminal behavior. How could they do otherwise, asked the advocates for maintenance? The culture from which they come has taught them that they are "dope fiends," that jails and asylums are filled with "drug wrecks," and that anyone who succumbs to such behavior must be inherently weak and somehow flawed.

---

[3] For a review of studies ranging from the late 19th century until 1940 regarding the psychopathic personality, see Maughs, 1941, 330–356, 465–499. For a review of the multitude of available treatments to "cure" drug addiction from the late 19th century until the mid-1920s, see Terry and Pellens, [1928], 1970, 517–628.

Pro-maintenance supporters argued that "there is no psychology of drug addiction." Rather, "the psychology of the drug addict is the psychology of the average human being" (Terry, 1921, 40–41). The pro-maintenance group was never in a dominant position, probably because they were promoting continued use of opiates during a time when reformers were positing the evils of drink and all drugs of pleasure.

Criminalization

In an effort to control the use of drugs, anti-narcotic legislation was passed at the local, state, federal, and international levels beginning in the late 19th century (Morgan, 1981; Musto, 1973; Terry and Pellens, [1928] 1970).

The idea that drug addiction was related to medical deficiencies may have inadvertently assisted those who sought legal control of narcotics by defining the problem as having a concrete solution—treatment and cure. If addiction was a disease and a cure was possible, the strict enforcement of anti-drug laws made sense. Once the present population of addicts was cured, the laws would naturally control further use. "The goal of strict enforcement is not so mysterious when one realizes that experts [of the time] believed that the addict, even if afflicted by a recognized and specific medical disease, only had to undergo . . . treatment to rid himself of the curse" (Musto, 1971, 605).

As laws were implemented to control drug use and fear about the dangers of addiction spread, the public could hardly help but see addicts as dangerous criminals. This view became increasingly accepted and widespread in the popular literature of the early 20th century. "The dope habit, unlike the drinking habit, the smoking habit or other habits, leads directly to crime" (Shepherd, 1923, 23).

What presumably made the perception of a drug addict especially frightening was that the use of drugs was said to be spreading. Addicts were becoming characterized as criminals who spread the habit to survive. A member of the 1923 New York narcotic squad reported that

> [N]o young man ever pays a cent for his first dose of heroin or cocaine. The first dose is always free. Someone always gives it to him to "cure" a headache, or to "pep him up" at a dance or a party or to give him "nerve" for some special occasion. Why does he get it free? Because every dope fiend tries to make dope fiends of all the persons around him. Every dope fiend has the constant horror of finding himself some day unable to get his drug; for this reason he associates with persons who use drugs and he tries to convert his friends into drug users. (Shepherd, 1923, 23)

Stories about this "horror," presumably related to the "atrocities" of which addicts were capable, were used to justify laws and social policy against drug use (Lindesmith, 1968).

By 1920, it was no longer possible to obtain opiates legally without a prescription from a doctor. The availability of narcotics and the numbers of medical and nonmedical addicts had also changed. In 1924, two doctors published a study noting that most addicts who now came to see them began their habits by associating with other users. In earlier times, these doctors pointed out, the most common reason for beginning drug use stemmed from health problems (Sceleth and Kuh, 1924).

The growing fear of addicts was nurtured by members of law enforcement agencies who typically stated that addiction caused crime and that addicts were a threat to society. A commissioner of corrections in New York expressed his view that "all drug addicts are criminals, either actual or potential, and there is no limit to their atrocities when deprived of their drug" (Wallis, 1925, 741). A U.S. district attorney claimed that though an addict "is a sick man . . . he is also a criminal and a menace to the community" (Kane, 1917, 502).

This anti-maintenance, pro-police ideology was perpetuated by high profile political figures such as Harry Anslinger, early head of the Federal Bureau of Narcotics, who strongly endorsed the view that the "treatment" of addicts should include separating them from society. A 1928 quote from Levi Nutt, Anslinger's predecessor, provides a representation of this perspective:

> As long as addicts are permitted to remain at liberty on the streets of our cities where they have access to the drugs they will continue to create a demand for smuggled narcotics. The isolation and segregation of addicts for institutional treatment under restraint for a long period of time will greatly reduce the spreading of drug addiction among our people, and largely destroy the existing demand for smuggled drugs. (quoted in Courtwright, 1982, 141)

In 1928, Congress approved the development of two narcotic "farms" or "hospitals" to be built in Lexington, Kentucky, and Fort Worth, Texas. These facilities became institutions where addicts could be incarcerated for law violations or treated on a voluntary basis. Lexington, which opened in 1935, resembled the penitentiaries being built at that time (Rasor, 1972) and can be seen as a major beginning for institutionalizing addicts. It is not surprising that authorities associated with the hospital reported high rates of success because doing otherwise might hinder their credibility (and funding). A 1937 *Time Magazine* article reported that "[t]he Lexington narcotic farm had admitted 1864 up to last week [and] discharged 1048 as physically cured of addiction" (*Time Magazine,* February 15, 1937, 70). Such success rates are deceptive. They imply that those who left the hospital "cured" would never again have a problem with heroin. For addicts, being "physically cured" usually means they will not find themselves going through withdrawal without the drug and nothing more. After "treatment" they typically begin using heroin again at some point, get addicted again, and have to go through the process all over again.

Another factor that affected perceptions of drug users was the outlawing of marijuana in the 1930s. This legislation was made possible, in part, by public hysteria generated by law enforcement authorities and racism against Mexicans in the Southwest (Sloman, 1979). Harry Anslinger led the crusade. The following exemplifies the type of propaganda he disseminated that helped bring about the change:

The sprawled body of a young girl lay crushed on the sidewalk the other day after a plunge from the fifth story of a Chicago apartment house. Everyone called it suicide, but actually it was murder. The killer was a narcotic known to America as marijuana . . . How many murders, suicides, robberies, criminal assaults, holdups, burglaries, and deeds of maniacal insanity it causes each year, especially among the young, can only be conjectured. The sweeping march of its addiction has been so insidious that, in numerous communities, it thrives almost unmolested, largely because of official ignorance of its effects. (Anslinger and Cooper, 1937, 18)

During the politically conservative1950s, while many Americans enjoyed the fruits of a flourishing economy and were confronted with the ramifications of communism, something else was stirring. In the streets of major cities, especially in the northeast, a recurring demon was rearing his ugly head. This time the beast was not only an addict, but also young and black.

Statistics, based on police arrests for narcotics and who was turning up at federal treatment centers during this period, indicated that the numbers of blacks becoming addicted to heroin were skyrocketing (Courtwright et al., 1989; Rasor, 1972). That such statistics are criticized for being biased is a valid but irrelevant argument. The fact is, politicians, law enforcement agencies, the media, and others with vested interests use such statistics to amplify social problems and shape public opinion. Based on this type of information, articles in the popular literature portrayed an epidemic of young, black heroin users.

Much of the data coming in about newly recruited black heroin addicts in the 1950s were valid and not to be downplayed. In the late 1940s, many blacks emigrated to cities in the north to attain what they believed would be decent jobs and living conditions. Many thought of the north as "the promised land." Instead, they were met with the horrid conditions of the inner city. Members of the underworld flooded black neighborhoods like Harlem with heroin—and many young people of the area used it to seek refuge from the situations of their lives (Brown, 1965).

Adding to the scare was the idea that drug addiction was spreading to the white middle class. One article stated that because of the declining numbers of addicts and the increasing supply of narcotics that emerged after World War II, "peddlers have left the slums and invaded middle-class schools and neighborhoods" (*Science Digest,* 1952, 34). Findings from studies indicated that more and more teenagers, not all of them black, were experimenting with a variety of substances as a form of rebellion (Ausubel, 1952; Morgan, 1981). This fearful scenario, typically blamed on drug peddlers, led to calls for stricter drug control legislation:

Prison sentences up to twenty years for narcotics sellers . . . were urged in an interim report on the problem of narcotics control . . . Frequent conferences with the Federal Narcotics Bureau, the New York Police Department and various agencies have emphasized the necessity of concentrating the attack of all law enforcement on the narcotics seller. (*New York Times,* February 8, 1951, P18[2])

Before long, lawmakers were seeking the death penalty for sales of heroin:

> A Senate investigating panel urged Congress today to authorize the death penalty for heroin smugglers and peddlers in extreme cases. These traffickers in "the most deadly" of narcotic drugs, Senator Price Daniel . . . told the Senate, were "selling murder, robbery and rape . . . Their offense is human destruction as surely as that of a murderer." (*New York Times,* January 10, 1956, P12[1])

The 1960s was a period of dramatic change in the United States. It was a time characterized by liberal and radical politics, sociological explanations for crime and addiction, civil rights activism, the Vietnam War, race riots in streets across the country and the countercultural/hippie movement that had drug use at its core. It was also the time when many of the fellas began getting high. Three things worth mentioning that can be related to conceptions of heroin addicts during this decade include high reported rates of drug use among Vietnam vets, grassroots attempts to help addicts, and the beginning of the "war on drugs."

Vietnam War Veterans

As the Vietnam War progressed from the early 1960s into the 1970s, stories of large-scale addiction among American soldiers surfaced in the U.S. press. Marijuana use was said to be rampant. It was estimated that 10 to 25 percent of enlisted men were using heroin. Like other problems from the American past, such as the threat of communism, the blame was placed on evil "foreigners." In this case, the Vietnamese enemy was corrupting "our boys." As in prior wars, large numbers of men were expected to be addicted upon their return to the United States. Rather than punishing them, which surely was not deserved because they were fighting for their country, the public supported rehabilitation programs as an alternative (Morgan, 1981).

Many of those who became addicted in Vietnam came from the same groups of young men who would have been prone to addiction if they hadn't gone overseas—young, poor, often nonwhite males. A classic study that looked at returning vets found that 88 percent of those addicted to heroin in Vietnam had not been addicted at any time in the three years following their return to the United States. According to those interviewed, the most common reasons for quitting was the high price of the drug and the difficulty in finding a steady supply (Robins, 1973). The study portrayed addiction as "situational" and is often cited to support law enforcement strategies of control (based on the idea that it proves high prices and low availability result in fewer addicts). However, the study contradicted the notion that addiction is related to individual psychopathological defects or criminality. Returning war veterans could hardly be portrayed as sick by their government. For a politician to suggest such a thing would be tantamount to political suicide. The experience and treatment of Vietnam War veterans who became involved with drug use is evidence that how the public sees addicts depends on who they are and how they are depicted within the wider society. In other words, how addicts are treated and, in turn, how they see themselves, is related more to social context than individual deficiencies.

Grassroots Treatment: Addicts Helping Addicts

The idea that drug addicts could turn their lives around by abstaining from the use of drugs gained acceptance by many, including addicts themselves, during the1960s. A milestone that helped reinforce this view can be traced to a therapeutic, live-in, drug treatment program called Synanon, created by Charles Dederich (himself a recovering alcoholic) in 1958. Synanon was a grassroots, non-law enforcement related program for heroin addicts that became a popular model for treatment facilities in the 1960s and1970s. These groups were usually situated in some old house or converted building. Participation was voluntary and free from the usual figures of authority, making it attractive to those who had an aversion to formal treatment.

Part of Synanon's popularity and acceptance by mainstream society was its emphasis on American values such as self-help, individualism, and the work ethic. Unfortunately, success rates from these programs were no better than any other methods of "curing" addicts. What has been shown is that while in a program, addicts have a chance to live a safe, structured life. Yet, once they leave, rates of relapse are high (Morgan, 1981; Walker, 2001, 268; Yablonsky, 1965).

Further grassroots efforts to help addicts were taking place in what, by the1960s, was known as Narcotics Anonymous (NA). The beginning of NA dates back to the 1940s and the efforts of a few addicts who were struggling to learn how to stay clean without the help of "experts." Borrowing from Alcoholics Anonymous (AA), they started weekly meetings called "Addicts Anonymous." These first meetings began in the hospital at Lexington in 1947 and continued until it closed in 1966[4] (Stone, 1997). Those who participated in these early meetings are credited with the development of Narcotics Anonymous. In 1953, there were only a handful of people attending one or two meetings in Los Angeles. NA today has approximately 20,000 groups worldwide, 16,000 of which are in the United States, with an estimated membership of 250,000 (Manchester, 1995).

Given that addicts were and are highly stigmatized, NA has had its ups and downs. For example, legislation enacted in New York in the 1960s (the Rockefeller laws) made it a felony for any drug addict on parole or probation to be seen in the presence of another addict. NA meetings in that state ceased to exist from then until the 1980s when these laws became ignored by police and addicts alike (Stone, 1997). Although there is no "proof" that NA "works," its tremendous growth can be seen as evidence of its popularity.

---

[4] In 1966, the hospital at Lexington "became part of the National Institute of Mental Health and its program emphasis was changed from treatment to research" (Stone, 1997, 4).

Like Synanon and AA, the organization of NA lies outside the net of the criminal justice system. However, it is common today for drug programs, judges, and parole officers to coerce their "clients" into attending NA or AA groups (see Goldman, 1998, for an example). In a recent interview on ABC's "Nightline," General Barry McCaffrey, then drug czar, called AA and NA "the best drug program in the world" ("Getting Straight," 1999). Perhaps more than anything else, the cultural awareness of 12-step programs and "recovery" from drugs and alcohol (shared by addicts and non-addicts alike) has helped perpetuate the idea that some addicts can and do quit using drugs. Although the notion that addicts can be "cured" is not new, the diffusion of the "success" of 12-step programs into the popular culture has perhaps created yet more pressure for people who use illegal drugs to alter their behavior. For those who want to quit, stories about people who do well by participating in AA or NA may provide hope. For those who want to continue using, these same stories may add to the likelihood that they see themselves as somehow flawed.

Politicizing Crime: The Beginning of the "War on Drugs"

During the1960s, the Civil Rights movement united millions of people in an effort to transform the status quo. Sit-ins, protests, marches, and confrontations with police were commonly seen on the nightly news. Whether the issue was racism, poverty, inequality, or the Vietnam War, the demand for change was difficult to ignore.

In response to the social upheaval, conservatives politicized crime and began efforts to convince the public that the real problem was a lack of law and order. They brought both the issue of crime and those defined as criminal, including illegal drug users, to the national level. Barry Goldwater, in his bid to become president in 1964, blamed the civil disorder on liberals, civil rights demonstrators, and criminal-coddling policies (Chambliss, 1999). Reducing poverty and inequality by implementing new laws and social programs, as suggested by liberals and radicals alike, was said to be unnecessary because the real problem was widespread immorality, dysfunctional lifestyles, and excessive permissiveness (Beckett and Sasson, 2000). These fear-generating views were at the heart of what would soon become a full scale "War on Drugs."

This tumultuous political landscape led to negative perceptions about illegal drug use that encompassed more than just heroin addicts. Getting high became extremely symbolic and a central feature of the countercultural, anti-establishment, anti-war, hippie movement made up of children (many of whom were attending college) of mainstream, white, middle-class America. Barbiturates, speed, and especially marijuana gained widespread popularity. To light up a joint was to oppose the war and the status quo. LSD, which was not illegal until late 1966, became an explosive threat. Taking drugs was a way of opposing authority. Michael Rossman, a member of the Berkeley Free Speech Movement, summarized it well:

> When a young person took his first puff of psychoactive smoke, he also
> drew in the psychoactive culture as a whole, the entire matrix of law and

association surrounding the drug, its induction and transaction. One in-
haled a certain way of dressing, talking, acting, certain attitudes. One
became a youth criminal against the State. (Lee and Shlain, 1985, 129)

The conservative perspective was strengthened among the many people
who were alarmed by culturally transmitted images of bra-less women and
stoned, long-haired people exhibiting behaviors that were far from the norm.
Marijuana and heroin came to be characterized in a similar light. *Newsweek*
magazine, for example, presented an article showing graphic photographs of
junkies overdosing in Harlem. On the same page, *Newsweek* quoted principals
saying they had discovered young teenagers smoking pot in the bathrooms of
their schools (*Newsweek,* April 21, 1969).

Such frightening images became valuable political capital. In his campaign
for the 1968 presidential election, Richard Nixon promised, if elected, to
combat the drug menace by accelerating the development of tools and
weapons to fight illegal drugs, triple the Customs Service, provide more federal drug agents, police, and anti-drug operations overseas. He kept his pledge.
Under his reign, the federal drug enforcement budget rose from $65 million
in 1969 to $719 million in 1974 (Baum, 1996). Gone were the days when the
addict stereotype was a person of color who used heroin, marijuana, or cocaine. Drugs, and more to the point, drug users of all racial and ethnic groups,
were now becoming the official scourge of politicians and law enforcement.

Even though drug users were increasingly stigmatized throughout the 1960s
and on into the 1970s, rehabilitation was still viewed by some as a sensible approach to dealing with addiction. For example, from roughly the mid-1960s to
the end of the 1970s, heroin addicts in California were commonly seen by ac-
tors in the criminal justice system as if they had a distinct, treatable, psychological problem. When an individual was arrested for a crime that could be linked
to drug addiction, courts often chose the option of sentencing that person to a
civil commitment at the California Rehabilitation Center (CRC) in Norco[5]—
an institution where several of the fellas served time. To get sent to CRC, which
was overseen by the same agency that oversees the state prisons—the California
Department of Corrections (CDC)—heroin users were interviewed by two psychiatrists who determined whether users were indeed addicts. If the court received psychiatric reports indicating an individual was an addict, he or she could
be given a sentence of 0 to 7 years at CRC. The commitment would be considered civil rather than criminal.[6] Success would mean the crime would be ex-
punged from one's record. Failure, which often resulted from the detection of
continued drug use or another crime, would result in another court appearance,
a criminal conviction for the exact same offense, and usually imprisonment.

---

[5] The CRC, modeled after the Lexington and Fort Worth hospitals, opened in 1961. Its
first director worked at Lexington in 1947 when the earliest Addicts Anonymous meetings
were being held (Stone, 1997, 45).

[6] Civil commitments were also used in New York and at the federal level. See Baum
(1996, 30) for a brief critique.

Beyond these legal distinctions, and the fact that people generally served shorter amounts of time if given a civil commitment, "rehabilitation" at CRC was really no different than "incarceration" in other medium security California prisons. Nothing about the institution was civil. Personally, it was the first place I ever did time for the state. The routinized lifestyle, monotony, racism, and violence in that facility were the same, as I would later see in other parts of the CDC.

As the years passed, the appeal of rehabilitation declined. Increasingly, people from all political persuasions criticized rehabilitation (Bayer, 1981). Conservatives opposed it because they felt punishment must be severe and painful to deter crime. Liberals began criticizing it as well, arguing that "open ended" or "indeterminate" sentences designed to "correct" led to discriminatory and arbitrary sentencing practices by individuals who were empowered to make release decisions (Beckett and Sasson, 2000).

California eliminated indeterminate sentencing laws in 1977, which, in essence, meant that the critique of the rehabilitation model was having a powerful effect. Suddenly, prison release dates were set by legislators rather than members of parole boards who, theoretically, based their decision on how well a prisoner did while in custody. The change meant that convicts would be given a specific (or determinate) rather than indeterminate amount of time (e.g., 5 years instead of 1 to 10 years) for their crimes. Other states and the federal government soon followed this lead. By the end of the decade, the belief was spreading across the culture that only the severe, sure threat of punishment would deter lawbreakers, including addicts. Rather than being seen as sick, or somehow flawed and in need of repair, addicts were increasingly being viewed as rational individuals who chose the course of their actions willingly and, therefore, deserved incarceration.

The "War on Drugs," which subsided somewhat during the Watergate hearings, the last years of the Vietnam War, and Jimmy Carter's presidency, returned in full force in the early 1980s and has been going strong ever since. Along with Ronald Reagan's ascendency to power during those years came a get-tough-on-crime agenda, which gained strength by focusing on issues related to illegal drugs. Like many of his conservative colleagues, Reagan argued that drug problems were a moral issue caused by bad people, not social conditions. Pushers were motivated by greed. Users were also to blame and should be held individually accountable (Beckett and Sasson, 2000).

The crack cocaine "epidemic," which emerged in the mid-1980s, acted as a springboard for increased hysteria about the drug menace. If the stories from the popular culture were to be believed, the very safety of the nation was at stake. In the earlier part of the decade, cocaine use was glamorized by television, movies, and literature that depicted well-to-do, white users snorting the drug for recreational purposes. By 1985, however, terror spread across the country as a proliferation of news stories defined the horrors of a new monster, crack cocaine.

It was said that the use of crack caused instant addiction and widespread violence. *Newsweek* magazine quoted the director of a cocaine hotline as saying,

"There is no such thing as recreational use of crack. Crack is the most addictive drug known to man right now" (quoted in Baum, 1996, 219). Adding to the fear of the supposed effects of the drug were illustrations of its users as black. Very quickly, crack was blamed on the deterioration of the country's inner cities, the killing of policemen, overburdened courts, overcrowded jails, and the well-being of children. Some commentators suggest that using crack to explain these social problems was, in reality, a racist-driven ploy (J. Miller, 1996, 63).

Once crack hit center stage, sensationalized news stories and "war-like," anti-drug rhetoric escalated dramatically. At the core of this attention was the idea that drug users are not accountable as human beings, and merit nothing less than condemnation and punishment. Thanks to Nancy Reagan, who equated drug use to homicide, "just say *no*," has come to mean just say no to drugs. "If you're a casual drug user," she claimed, "you're an accomplice to murder" (Roberts, 1988, A16). Mirroring her sentiments, President Bush (senior) once said, "Casual drug use is responsible for the casualties of the drug war" (Bush, 1990, 1180). In 1990, Los Angeles police chief Daryl Gates made a comment to the Senate that "casual drug users should be taken out and shot" (Norris et al., 1998, 6). President Reagan, like his wife, was quick to ostracize drug users. At one time, he claimed, "We will no longer tolerate those who sell drugs and those who buy drugs. All Americans of good will are determined to stamp out those parasites" (Reagan, 1991, 1311).

The fear of crack cocaine within the wider context of the "War on Drugs" and get-tough-on-crime political rhetoric helped establish and justify a steady stream of new laws, increased expenditures on crime control, lengthier sentences for nearly all types of crimes, and mandatory minimum sentences for drug offenders. Among other things, these actions have empowered prosecutors, taken discretion away from judges, and disproportionately affected poor, urban communities. Democrats as well as Republicans have jumped on the bandwagon. In 1994, President Clinton signed a bill giving nearly $24 billion to local law enforcement agencies to add 100,000 new police officers and $7.9 billion to construct new state prisons (Chambliss, 1999, 25–27).

Cumulatively, these forces helped create the massive imprisonment binge (Austin and Irwin, 2001), which has grown exponentially in the past two decades in the United States. In sheer numbers, we have gone from incarcerating just over 300,000 people in 1980 (Maguire and Pastore, 1999, 490) to an estimated 2 million in March 2000 (Katz, 2000). Governmental support for the prosecution of drug offenders, most of which are nonwhite, is one of the largest factors affecting this expansion. A study conducted by Human Rights Watch concluded, "Drug control policies bear responsibility for the quadrupling of the national prison population since 1980 and a soaring incarceration rate" (Human Rights Watch, 2000). From 1980 to 1997, the numbers of people sent to prison for drug offenses nationally increased eleven-fold (up 1040 percent) while those imprisoned for violent crimes nearly doubled (up 82 percent). At the time of this writing, nearly one in four imprisoned in the United States is doing time for a drug offense. In California, 44,455 of the current

160,000 plus prison population are drug offenders—a higher percentage than in any other state (Schiraldi et al., 2000).

Locking up so many people serves many political and economic interests (Austin and Irwin, 2001; Parenti, 1999). Yet, it also has negative effects on communities, families, and individuals. One of the unintended, usually over-looked consequences of current policies that result in the incarceration of mass numbers of human beings (including drug offenders), is the creation of a huge class of individuals who see themselves as different from "normal" people. The development of this "us" versus "them" distinction often worsens the very problems that social policies are supposedly designed to resolve (Terry, 2000). It had a strong impact on the lives of the men interviewed for this study.

SUMMARY

From this brief examination of the social construction of drug addiction as deviant, criminal, or both, it is easy to see some fundamental sociological principles at work that have intensified the problem and affected the self-concepts of drug users. First, addiction was stigmatized. Second, it became a "serious" social problem that, as it was given more and more attention, be-came increasingly fearful and threatening to the public (adding more stigma). Third, laws were implemented to "control" or "treat" the problem. These laws resulted in criminal sanctions against opiate use and imprisonment for "offenders" who, in turn, have become the exemplars of all addicts. As this process of dealing with the problem became normalized over time, so too have the cultural beliefs about what it means to be an addict. The social con-struction of addiction, then, has resulted in the development of a stereotypi-cal image of an addict.

That illegal drugs are dangerous and users of those drugs need to be im-prisoned (because they are criminal) or rehabilitated (because they are sick), or both, is so well established today that it can almost be seen as a cultural arti-fact. This impression is relentlessly reinforced in the popular culture with frightening images that seldom provide a valid representation of all the people who get high. Videotape from the news media, for example, is seldom (if ever) used to film factory workers ingesting an illegal stimulant to get them through their shift, or unwinding on a Monday night by smoking marijuana. The mainstream culture never gets exposed to pictures of stockbrokers, doctors, lawyers, college professors, or business executives, all people who are greatly admired, relaxing with an illegal drug at bedtime. We do not see pictures of neat working-class neighborhoods, huge mansions, or giant commercial en-terprises that are environments of typical illegal drug users. "Instead, we see images of slums, human degradation, and heavily armed police storming a drug house" (R. Miller, 1996, 21). In reality, illegal drug users (most whom are white) with jobs and stakes in the mainstream culture are seldom detected. If caught, they often get sent to treatment programs paid for with insurance policies. Everyone else gets placed within the jurisdiction of the criminal justice system.

The next chapter introduces the fellas. I also illustrate the differences found among them regarding their childhoods, early drug use, and initial experiences and interpretations of incarceration.

3

The Fellas:
Early Pathways Toward
Addiction and
Incarceration

The other day I had the opportunity to visit with five of my young nephews whose ages range from 5 to 12. They know about my past—that I've been to prison and used drugs and all. But, like most people who know I am clean and "doing good" today, they do not seem to hold it against me. We were sitting in a restaurant, and I asked them what they wanted to do when they grew up. Their answers, which reflected their religion-oriented home lives, included hopes of being a preacher, a missionary, and a police officer. After their responses I inquired, somewhat jokingly, "You mean none of you guys want to be a drug addict?" They yelled back, "No!" Then I said, "Or a convict?" Again, I heard a resounding, "No!" Their laughter filled the room. The idea of growing up to be a convict or a drug addict does not seem like something any kid would really anticipate. I know I didn't. Yet, my research showed me that some youngsters, at the ages of or younger than those of my oldest nephews, are already using drugs and getting locked up. Moreover, they do not typically think that what they are doing is funny or beyond belief.

This chapter introduces the fellas as they were at the time of the interviews and looks at their younger years. The focus is on where they came from and their early periods of drug use and incarceration. As well as providing a pseudonym and brief story about each of the men, I included their respective ages, race, number of years spent behind bars, and lengths of clean time. My hope is that this information will bring their humanity to life and enhance the readability of the rest of the book.

As I analyzed the data collected from the interviews, I found three distinct groups that, while growing up, had different life experiences and ways of evaluating themselves. Men from the first group were more or less born into it—they came from environments in which breaking the law, violence, and using drugs was the norm. The second group often came from similar socio-economic backgrounds, but grew up around people who embraced less deviant values. They claimed aspirations of being like those from the first group; they wanted to be the "hard guy." Finally, there were those who "wore many hats" as youngsters—some conventional, some deviant. They came from middle-class backgrounds and drifted into lives of addiction and criminality. I call these groups "regulars" (or "regs"), "wannabes," and "drifters" respectively. Classifying them in this way proved useful as a descriptive and analytical tool. However, a note should be made that though these categories were discovered among the fellas, they do not necessarily reflect what might be found within a larger population of men with similar backgrounds.

The reasons given by the men from each of these groups regarding what influenced their initial "ways in" to heroin addict lifestyles and what they gained by doing so varied. Their narratives illustrate differences in the development of their early self-concepts and behavior.

REGULARS

Regulars were the group of guys who, as children, grew up in social settings where illegal drug use, crime, violence, and spending time in prison were not uncommon. Eight of the 20 men fit these criteria. As youths, they became involved in a "street culture" characterized as rebellious, violent, and resistant to mainstream values (Bourgois, 1995). I use the term *regular* (or *reg*) because it is the name prisoners use to refer to those who are seen as "the elite of the convict world. A 'regular' . . . can be counted on by other regulars . . . is level-headed [and has] guts" (Irwin, 1970, 83).

To a large degree, the lives of the young regulars were shaped by a need to gain respect by peers, members of their community and, perhaps most importantly, themselves. Much like the youth in Elijah Anderson's (1999) study of Philadelphia's inner-city, they became involved in an "oppositional culture" characterized by a "code of the street." Within this context, which stems from a deep-felt sense of alienation from mainstream society, respect is earned by being seen as a "bad ass" (Katz, 1988, 80), dangerous, violent, and afraid of nothing—not even death. By participating in and identifying with this "street" culture, the regulars could be looked upon favorably by others. From this standpoint, being a regular and adhering to the values of the street are virtually synonymous.

The importance of respect in relation to the code of the streets needs to be emphasized. Culturally, as in America's ghettos and barrios, the code evolved from the pervasive despair related to the general circumstances of life that include the stigma of race, blocked opportunities, rampant violence, endemic drug addiction and hopelessness (Anderson, 1999, 32–33). Individually, the development of the self as "bad," which is common in but not limited to such environments, often occurs when people are continuously treated with contempt or rejected. In either case, that is, culturally or individually, respect is lacking. Conforming to the mores of the street and presenting oneself as a regular is a means of filling that void. Regarding the meaning of this respect, Anderson suggests it is a valuable form of social capital that not only serves as a means of protection but also helps form "the core of the person's self-esteem, particularly when alternative forms of self-expression are closed or sensed to be" (Anderson, 1999, 66). In other words, the code allows them to develop and maintain a positive self-evaluation.

Who They Were

Huero was a white, 46-year-old who grew up around Mexican Americans. Altogether, he had spent about 15 years behind bars. When we met, he had 35 days of clean time, and was living in a residential drug program that I will call Hope House. Underneath the hardened image he had been presenting to the world for decades, I sensed a frightened individual who saw himself at a crossroads in his life. During the interview, he expressed regrets about his past, compassion for others—especially children, and fear about his future, which seemed to surface from a lack of confidence in himself. He was very aware that although he knew how to thrive in the worlds of heroin addicts and prison, he knew little else.

Baggy was a 46-year-old Chicano who was raised around 11 brothers and sisters. Altogether, he had been incarcerated nearly five years of his life. Our social worlds overlapped at times, so I had seen Baggy now and then for more than 20 years. Like Huero, Baggy was living at Hope House when we met for the interview and had managed to stay clean for eight months at that time. Unlike most of the other regulars, Baggy usually managed to hold down a job. Often, when his drug habit would get too bad, he would get clean for brief periods. His ability to work and quit using heroin when things started looking bleak likely helped reduce the amount of time he spent in prison. Before we got started on the interview, I mentioned Bongo, a mutual acquaintance, who had just been arrested for bank robbery. Bongo, who had only been out of prison for a few weeks, robbed a bank in a busy part of town in the middle of the day. After stuffing the money into his pants, he made his getaway on a bicycle. Within minutes, he ran a red light right in front of a police car and was subsequently arrested. Last I heard, he was sentenced to something like 30 years. Baggy had heard the story. All he could say was, "I hate shit like that. I seen him not long ago. He was doing good at the Salvation Army, working as a baker. And now this. Man, he's through, huh?" Yeah, he's through.

Pelon was a 47-year-old Chicano who had spent 18 years in custody. I first met Pelon at NA meetings in the early 1990s. Soon thereafter, I saw him working in the kitchen at the community college I was attending. Like me, he was given a work-study job to help pay his bills while attending school. It was nice having him there back then. Seeing him in the cafeteria, or on the campus somewhere always gave me a boost. Just the presence of someone I knew with a similar background eased my own struggle with adapting to the outside world. He gave me inspiration, hope, a sense of connection, and the feeling that I was not alone. Quiet, bald-headed, and in tremendous physical condition, he had been clean for seven years at the time of the interview.

Jumbo was a 58-year-old Chicano who had done seven years behind bars and had six years of clean time when we met. He told me he picked up the name Jumbo in Soledad, a California prison, in the 1960s because he was extremely overweight. After he shed more than a hundred pounds by playing handball everyday, the name got shortened to "Jo." To interview Jumbo, I met with him at his job on three different occasions. Employed by the local police department, he worked at a drop-in detox shelter for alcoholics in the skid row area of town. As I sat and watched him interact with others who came in and out of the small facility, I noticed how he was treated with respect. Not the type of respect earned by projecting an image of fearlessness, but one that was genuine. By the time our meetings were over, it was clear to me that Jumbo had a kind, caring heart and would do nearly anything to lend a hand to someone needing help.

Wheels was a white, 46-year-old with 11 years clean who had spent 15 years in prison. Though I never got to know him personally, I first saw Wheels in the penitentiary in the mid-1980s rolling around the institution in a wheelchair, his shriveled body wracked by some type of ailment the doctors apparently could not treat. Because of his vibrant health and the positive disposition he projected before the interview even began, it was easy to assume that his self-concept had indeed changed dramatically since those long-gone days in prison. My assumptions were validated ten times over by the time I heard his story.

Sticks was a black, 49-year-old. Before his 4 years of clean time, he spent more than 19 years in custody. Like Jumbo, he worked at a detox center. Like Wheels, I did not know Sticks even though we were incarcerated in the same penitentiary at the same time. Ironically, we both attended college classes within that prison and were influenced by some of the same teachers. My introduction to Sticks, in fact, was made by one of those teachers years after being paroled. Sometimes, it really does seem like a very small world.

Weasel was a 61-year-old Mexican who had accumulated 8 years of clean time. Altogether, he had spent roughly 12 years in jail and prison. As with several of the other fellas, I met Weasel while attending NA meetings. In fact, we both got clean within a few months of each other. As time passed, we became good friends. Like Pelon and me, Weasel ended up attending classes at the local community college. While there, he worked as a counselor in one of the school's programs that helped people who came from low-income and disadvantaged backgrounds. Because of his insightfulness and sense of humor, spending time with Weasel was always fun. Once, when we were together, I had to pull the car I was driving off the road because it was overheating. After pulling to a stop, he got out and approached the hood, expecting me to somehow open it from where I was sitting behind the wheel. Unfortunately, I did not know how to accomplish such a complicated task. During the several minutes it took us to figure out how to open the damn thing, amidst profanities that would have made a truck driver blush, we nearly hurt ourselves from laughing so hard.

Kickstand was a white, 46-year-old who, before staying clean for 90 days, had spent more than 25 years behind bars. When we met, he was at Hope House with Huero and Baggy. His body covered with tattoos, part of one leg missing from the knee down, Kickstand seemed reluctant to consent to an interview. At that time, he was still adjusting to being clean and living outside prison with others (few he could relate to) in a treatment-oriented environment. Once he let down his guard, however, what emerged was an extremely good and often comically natured human being who was a joy to be around. At one point, he told me the reason he lost part of his leg was that he got shot. After I expressed regret for his loss, he said, "Well, one thing I learned from that little adventure is you don't bring a knife to a gunfight."

Where They Came From

The most common characteristic of the regulars as youngsters was their exposure to role models and environments where violence, drug addiction, trips to prison, and poverty were often the norm. That they developed self-concepts as deviant or "bad" individuals, and, over time, became regs in prison, began to make sense while I listened to episodes from their youth. Their words indicated that they had been regulars-in-the-making from a very early age.

Several of the regs learned early on that acting violently was a way of dealing with problems. As children, they were often objects of violence. They commonly spoke of being physically abused. Two admitted they were victims of rape. Weasel, who grew up in a town rooted in poverty and illegal activity just south of the California border, said that most of his memories as a young child were related to being severely beaten. "What I remember about from birth to say seven years old—a lotta poverty, lotta ass whipping. The whippings weren't spankings, they were beatings." The beatings, which came from a brother-in-law who acted as a father, frightened him and hindered his ability to communicate with his family. "One time I fell and hit my head at school. I didn't wanna tell my family 'cause I knew they would whip me. I was vomiting, eyes crossed, had cold sweats, and didn't say anything for three days." From the way he was treated, he learned that hurting people was acceptable, normal behavior. As he aged, he became friends with others in his neighborhood who shared similar backgrounds. They confirmed his view that violence was good and provided him with validation, social support, and a sense of well being.

Learning to settle disputes by fighting was typical behavior among the regs when they were young. It was a way of gaining prestige within the neighborhood. Huero told me that from the age of five, he was encouraged to fight by his pachuco[1] uncles and validated for his efforts. "I guess with the fighting I got recognition from them." He then talked about having to switch schools when he got a little older. The transition from a public to a Catholic school was difficult. Yet, it was not the school so much as it was the new kids that he saw as burdensome. He said the children at his old school were, like him, mostly poor "and everything was cool." But the kids at the Catholic school came from families with money and prestige. Seeing himself differently was alienating and affected his developing resistance to mainstream values:

> The kids had dads that were doctors or they worked as scientists at the air force base. They could'a been lying but that's what they said. And my dad was driving a shit truck for Granite [asphalt construction company], emptying out the toilets on construction sites.

To alleviate his feelings of inferiority, he used violence to gain a sense of dignity and control:

> So I felt less. But there was one way I wasn't less. I'll kick the shit out of 'em. So I'm fighting. Beating up these rich kids. And they didn't dig it at that school. I'm coming to school, my clothes are dirty 'cause my mom works all day. She ain't got time. And I feel inferior, you know. So the only way I could—you know, was fuck your school. I'll show you, fuck you nuns and all this shit.

Fighting became a way of dealing with problems with which he was familiar and that had previously brought him prestige. His actions were a reaction—secondary deviation as noted by Lemert (1996)—to his stigmatization brought about because he dressed poorly and wore dirty clothes in a new school. His perception of being seen by other kids as "less" helped him further develop and reinforce his self-concept as a bad person. Thus, he dealt with his feelings of alienation and inferiority by being violent. Hurting those who he perceived to be the cause of his negative self-images was a way of counteracting the pain. When acting with anger and violence, he felt powerful, strong, and right. For many young regs, the ability to fight became a positive, self-defining characteristic.

The abundance of deviance in the environments where the regs grew up provided them with niches they could fall into, ways of seeing the world, and styles of behavior that were contrary to mainstream norms. As Edwin Sutherland pointed out long ago, if everyone you know has deviant values, chances are you will develop deviant values as well (Sutherland, 1939). Weasel, for example, said that as a youngster he was surrounded by illegal activities. "This neighborhood where I lived happened to be where everything was happening, famous for prostitution, drug dealing, robberies—you name it." By the time he was 12 or 13, he was immersed within this deviant social world. "I

---

[1] "The second [Mexican immigrant] generation in the 1930s–1940s developed the pachuco lifestyle (a label created for those who wore zoot suits and spoke a mixed English-Spanish slang language)" (Vigil, 1988, 6). They represented a specific form of an oppositional culture.

just fell right into it," he remembered. By then his hair and style of clothes deviated from the societal norm. By dressing in this manner, he was extending the culture he learned in his neighborhood. His style was an indicator of his "bad" perspective (Katz, 1988) and a symbol of his connection with the street.

For young regs, spending time behind bars was a familiar, normal type of activity. At early ages, they often knew about people in their neighborhoods who were sent away to do time in prison, and they visited older relatives inside prison walls. In fact, many of their role models were ex-convicts. The young life of Baggy is illustrative. He came from a large, relatively poor family, and never knew his father. "My father figures were my brothers. They were all state raised," he told me. A *state-raised* individual is one who began his or her incarcerated experiences as a youth.[2] His brothers took him places as a youngster and exposed him to many of the symbols that represented their deviant perspectives. "I remember they used to tag me along with them. I remember a lot of '54 Chevies, low riders, oldies [music] and stuff like that—and dudes coming from out of town. You know, sunglasses, khakis, and all that shit." Being exposed to, and influenced by, people who had spent time in prison provided the young regs with a sense of direction and a glimpse into their own, not too distant futures.

Early Drug Use

Drug use was common in the youthful social worlds of the regs. Several began drinking alcohol before they were 10 years old. Kickstand, for example, was arrested for being drunk in public at the age of nine. They were typically surrounded by people, often members of their families, who used illegal drugs such as marijuana, barbiturates, and heroin. Before they tried heroin themselves, most of them had already been regularly drinking alcohol and smoking marijuana. Several went through periods in which they sniffed glue. They also commonly took prescription pills or LSD.

The regs' heroin use usually began at ages ranging from 12 to 15 and was often affected by relationships they had with older males whom they admired. For most of them, heroin use was not viewed as anything exceptionally abnormal when compared with other drug related activities. Weasel, for example, told me that his initial use of heroin began simply because it was available. It was one of many drugs that people he knew in his neighborhood were using. The meaning he gave to these associations, more than to the drug, affected his outlook during this period. "To me we were the same, whether we were using stuff [heroin], reds, weed or anything else. We thought of ourselves as vato locos[3]—crazy dudes." His central means of identification, like many Chicano youth who are labeled as gang members in southern California today

---

[2] For more on "state-raised youth" see Irwin, 1970, 26–29.

[3] "Locura is a state of mind where various actions bordering on 'craziness' take place. A loco exhibits this mind set by alternately acting tough, fearless and daring and by exhibiting other spontaneous types of behavior, such as getting 'loco' on drugs and alcohol" (Vigil, 1988, 166).

(Vigil, 1988), revolved around being a vato loco–a peculiar form of opposi-tional culture also associated with the street.

The regs often began using heroin when they were youngsters because they did not want to be seen as outsiders. Their friends, cousins, and brothers were often addicts. They often saw older males who used heroin with eyes of adoration. Baggy recalled his early impression of some of the men he looked up to when he first started fixing.[4] "They were always in trouble, hiding be-hind shades, always locked up and they were heroin addicts." He continued by telling me that the main reason he tried the drug was that he was sur-rounded by friends who were using it and he did not want to be viewed as different or scared. "What happened was the first time I shot heroin was to get into the gang. It was like if you got any heart, you'll fix this heroin, you know?" Not having any heart means being afraid. According to the values of the street, fear is a forbidden trait. So he, like many of the other regs, tried the drug to avoid stigmatization and express conformity within a deviant so-cial world.

Heroin was readily available to the young regs. As youngsters, they were exposed to older males who had been to prison and who sold heroin as a means to support their habits. One of the reasons they admired these older in-dividuals was because they viewed them as men who led fearless, exciting lives as outlaws. The young regs were familiar to the older men, who tended to treat them with decency and respect. These men also often offered the young-sters some of the drug for free. Huero, for example, told me that his introduc-tion to heroin, at the age of 15, came about because he had a girlfriend whose older brothers were heroin addicts who sold the drug to maintain their habits. "They were old dope fiends in this town." Their source of the drug was Mex-ico and, at times, they had a plentiful supply. "Sometimes I'd go over there and see big dinner plates of it out on the table." They offered him some sev-eral times and, even though he was afraid, he finally tried it. His positive view of these older men and a desire to look good in their eyes likely influenced his decision. "I mean, they're loaded, nice to everybody. I felt accepted by these guys." As do many beginning heroin users, he got sick to his stomach follow-ing his first few highs. "After I finally tried a little bit, I got sick as a dog. Was puking." Once the bouts of having an upset stomach became a thing of the past, he fell in love with the way the drug made him feel. "It was way better than glue. And fuck weed. Fuck booze. LSD? Fuck all that. And that's when I started. I was 15, almost 16." As well as make him feel good, his eventual reg-ular use of heroin became another form of resistance central to his member-ship in the social world of the street.

The opiate habits of the regulars did not all begin with drugs from illegal sources. Sticks, like most addicts in the 19th century, began using morphine for medical reasons. His introduction to the drug came about during a hospi-tal stay. At the time, his health was hampered because his mother, a prostitute,

---

[4] For heroin addicts, the term "fixing" refers to the process of injecting the drug into their bodies.

tried to abort him by taking strange chemicals and throwing herself down some stairs before he was born. He claimed that during his childhood she and his father, who was often in prison, beat him regularly. "I don't know if the beatings came from feelings of resentment over things I did or over me just being born. But I was brutalized." At the age of 15, he moved away from home and began living with a prostitute. Though he helped her by delivering drugs she was selling to customers, his own use did not begin until a year later when he was admitted to a hospital for surgery:

> As a result of my childhood stuff my body was deformed and so they took and gave me surgery. They called it spinal fusion. I was in the hospital for three months. Three times a day I was given injections of morphine and that's where my disease kicked in.

There, he learned that morphine eased both his physical and emotional pain:

> I noticed that while I was high the emotional stuff deadened. I was feeling lonely about being in the hospital at that time, but when I was under the influence of morphine it didn't matter. It didn't matter about my girl-friend—and I had a son at that time—and it didn't matter about what they were doing or why they weren't coming to see me.

His appreciation of the drug came about during a low point in his life. His feelings of loneliness and abandonment left him with a low self-image. This negative self-evaluation may have had a lot to do with his perception of the effect of the drug. Interestingly, though he had been around drugs all his life, not until his hospital stay did he become involved in their use. In other words, his drug use began when he hit an emotional bottom. His perception of its effects likely reflected the values of his environment. He came from a place where drugs were seen as good. They were also commonly and openly sought. His background then, predisposed him to accept the drug. It was not long after leaving the hospital that he found himself in prison for charges that stemmed from a relationship he had with a prostitute and his drug-related activities. "Before I knew it I was in prison a lot and my friends were all regulars." The regulars he associated with behind bars were not much different than people he knew on the outside. Both social worlds reflected the same values. By then, the script for his future was basically set.

Early Incarceration

The ways the three groups of men experienced early periods of incarceration reflects the environments from which they came and their self-evaluations. Of the three, the regulars had the least amount of difficulty "doing time." In fact, for most, the prison world was a place where they could shine.

The regs often mentioned that they actually enjoyed being locked up as juveniles. Wheels talked about making the transition from being a kid who slept with his mother while he was in junior high school to a prisoner in juvenile hall. He found the experience to be rewarding:

I went right from peeing my bed into juvenile hall in LA. Toughest guys in the land go there when they're that old. And I didn't pee the bed no more. When I went to jail at 12, I liked it. I was a success there. I learned it was a place where I could connive and make it and there was a certain quality of safeness in the institution.

The young regs had the social tools to survive in prison because of their familiarity with street values. These gave them an advantage, a sense of superiority, and status over those who lacked knowledge about the worlds behind bars. Their ability to negotiate safely in such an upside-down environment offered them a sense of power. Huero explained that he was not like some prisoners who find their first trip behind bars to be a miserable experience. He was not like some who might be assaulted sexually. It was easy for him to survive inside because he knew the language, the games, and how to act. In short, he saw himself as a regular. "I was just one of the fellas, one of the guys. I felt like somebody," he remembered. While incarcerated he could act violently and be validated by others for his efforts. He told me that when novices to the jail environment entered, he would experience an increased sense of well being. "I felt like, yeah, you're coming into my area now. And I'm king of this castle."

The regs often already knew people in the prisons to which they were assigned. Pelon, for example, who came from a poor, segregated, Mexican American community, said he never had much difficulty being locked up as a juvenile because he always had friends there from his neighborhood. "It really wasn't that different than when I was out. I mean, because the same guys I hung around with out here were in there." Though the regs could obviously not do all the things they did on the outside while they did time, the norms and meanings of their home neighborhoods differed little compared with the ones they lived with behind bars.

WANNABES

The second ideal type that emerged are what I call wannabes—individuals who made it clear during their interviews that, as youngsters, they aspired to be like regs. In other words, they "wanted to be" seen as regulars. Three of the 20 men fit this category. The term "wannabe" is used in a variety of contexts, including prison and drug-using cultures, by people with status in reference to others who are seen as outsiders trying to fit within their groups. It is an expression used in law enforcement circles to refer to people who want to be cops or gang members (Parsons and Jesilow, 2001), by gangs themselves to describe recruits (Shelden et al., 2001), and by Chicanos in East Los Angeles high schools to belittle recently arrived immigrants who have not yet taken on the aspects of the local culture (Katz, 1988).

Who They Were

Junior was a 52-year-old Chicano who had spent 7 years behind bars. At the time we met, he had been clean for 12 years. Junior came into my life almost by accident. I had met his brother, who I'll call Henry, in my first year at city college after getting out of prison in 1990. Henry and I hit it off because we shared similarities that set us apart from most of the other students. For one thing, we were older. Beyond that, we both had firsthand experience with the street. Unlike me, though, Henry managed to pull himself out of that lifestyle by entering the military after he left high school. Several years after those early college days, I ran into Henry in the library at a university campus where he was working as a security guard. We then spent several minutes catching up on what each of us had been doing since we had last met. When I told him about the research I was doing for this book and the type of people I was looking for to interview, he suggested I contact his brother who, as he said, "was one of those guys." Gratefully, I jotted down the number, gave Junior a call, and set up a meeting. I only got together with Junior once, in the back of an unused office area where my wife worked. But his story proved especially useful. Of all the fellas, he was the only one who had never been involved in 12-step programs. He did, however, spend about a year in a residential drug program that helped him turn his life around.

Bigwood was a white, 42-year-old who, after spending about 8 years behind bars, had been clean for 13 months when we got together for the interview. I ran into him on several occasions when we both were visiting people at Hope House. Baggy, who knew him for years, introduced us one day, and we hit it off immediately. Bigwood also knew Huero, who once told me that the support and encouragement he got from both Bigwood and Baggy was one of the major reasons he had decided to get into the program in the first place and give it a try. These guys had used heroin together, spent time in prison together, and were now trying to help each other stay clean.

Doctor Dee was a white, 44-year-old with 5 years clean who had spent roughly 9.5 years in custody. He mentioned picking up this nickname when he was a youngster because addicts who could not inject (fix) narcotics themselves often sought his help because of his ability to accomplish the task. With unquestioned faith, they stuck out their arms for him to poke with a needle, and, once a vein was found, shoot the drug into their bodies. We met through a mutual acquaintance, and saw each other now and then at 12-step meetings. Like me, and several of the other fellas, Doctor Dee was pursuing a formal education at the time of the interview.

Where They Came From

Compared with the regulars, the wannabes did not grow up surrounded by illegal drug use and criminality. As youngsters, however, they typically learned that taking actions that were contrary to middle-class values could lead to being admired and accepted by others. In other words, they discovered that there were times when being "bad" was good.

Wannabes may have been marginalized as youngsters and sought the world of the regulars as a means of gaining acceptance. Bigwood told me that he came from a "nice, strong Catholic family." He was the youngest of six siblings. His father worked two jobs and was a harsh disciplinarian. "Seemed like I was always getting spanked," he remembered. He saw his mother as characteristic of many women of the 1950s and 1960s. She took care of the kids and the house. "Moms was always a protector," he told me. He felt like an outsider at a very young age. His brothers, who called him Shadow and hid from him, kept him apart from their activities. By the time he entered school, he was teased for being clumsy and big for his age. Within a few years, he began to discover that doing things that contradicted normal expectations and demands could result in him being validated as "good" by other kids. He said he began cussing, putting cherry bombs in toilets, and pulling fire alarms. "And now everybody likes me 'cause I'm bad." His parents and teachers would tell him he was a good kid and ask him why he was being bad. He was unable to tell them that his actions were related to the positive reinforcement he was receiving from other kids. "I was being bad because my peers were making me happy." After getting kicked out of Catholic school for cussing out a priest, he entered public school and once again felt different because he thought other kids were looking at him as an outsider. "I thought they looked at me like I was a nerd, or a little Catholic boy—not as good as them. I felt scared, you know, had a lot of fear about it." Before long he got suspended violating school regulations. Soon thereafter, a couple kids from the class approached him to ask if he wanted to hang out with them for awhile. Their friendliness was welcome, and he was glad for the offer. As it turned out, they too frequently broke the rules.

Perhaps the central characteristic of the wannabes was that they found those defined here as regulars to have an appealing lifestyle and way of being. Further, when the wannabes compared themselves to regs, they often felt inadequate. Junior made it clear that from a very early age he wanted to be different. He too came from a large, religious family; in addition to his parents, he had 12 brothers and sisters. As a youngster, Junior attended Catholic school where he excelled in athletics and was looked up to by others. Yet in his neighborhood there were certain kids he saw as having superior qualities. For years, he wished they were characteristics he could call his own. "They had something better than the self-esteem I had. They had something I wanted. Since early childhood I always wanted to identify with them." These were kids who were getting in trouble with the law. They were the ones wearing clothes and talking in ways that set them apart from other youngsters. "They were a delinquent element. They had recognition." On occasion, he felt self-conscious and humiliated while in their presence. "I would be embarrassed that they would see me in my private Catholic school," he remembered.

Early Drug Use

As with most of the other fellas, the wannabes were introduced to drugs and alcohol by their peers. They typically began getting high early in life, drinking alcohol and smoking marijuana by the time they were 12 or 13. Because of their environments, however, their access to drugs, particularly heroin, was not as easy as it was for the regs.

The wannabes' willingness to experiment with drugs was a symbol of their rebelliousness and their desire to be like regulars. This was especially the case when it came to trying heroin. After all, using illegal drugs was symbolic of behavior that contradicted mainstream norms and was highly stigmatized. People who used drugs were "bad." Doctor Dee talked about how in the 1960s he had an attraction toward drug users in his school who were, because of the nature of their actions, lawbreakers. "You know, that reckless crowd had an appeal at that age." By the time he was in high school, he had been drinking alcohol and smoking pot for several years. When he was 17, a friend brought some heroin home from Vietnam. He smoked some of it, liked it, and began taking actions that were consistent with the norms of the drug-using subculture. "I kinda got caught up in that drug underworld. I started selling reds [barbiturates]. Started making quick bucks." His drug-selling activities took him deeper into the social world of the street. As his participation in this "drug underworld" progressed, so did his admiration for the regulars. He told me, "My role models and heroes became the guys—I thought they were so cool man—they'd been to the pen, they came home with tattoos, they drove low cars, had fine looking women." To emulate them, he developed a conscious desire to follow in their path:

> I wanted to be just like that. And they all shot heroin. So somewhere in my senior year I took my first fix and I liked it. At the beginning I don't think it was so much a love for the drug as it was the lifestyle and the crowd I was in with.

He revered the regs he met along the way and saw them as the epitome of rebellion and autonomy. "I just thought they were the John Waynes of the 1970s, the real men."

Using heroin properly was evidence that helped solidify membership in the culture of the street. Respondents in all three categories mentioned that when they first began using heroin they had a tendency to vomit after using the drug. Junior equated his initial bouts of sickness with his self-concept. He told me about how managing to use the drug without throwing up was yet another symbol of status and inclusion. "Once you didn't throw up anymore after your first initial fixes, you were in. You were somebody then. After you could fix and not throw up and eat—then you were mature. You had reached it."

Both regulars and wannabes attained some degree of status among their peers when they began using heroin. The difference is that the wannabes were always trying to be like what the regs already were.

Early Incarceration

Unlike the regulars, who generally claimed it was not difficult to do time when they were young, wannabes had to make more adjustments to incarcerative living. They were not as familiar with prison stories told by family members and friends. As youngsters, they were not raised in neighborhoods where people commonly went to prison.

Wannabes generally experienced feelings of fear, guilt, and awe during their first trips behind bars. They were frightened because of the alien nature of the places they were sent, which included harsh living conditions, guards who treated prisoners disrespectfully, and other prisoners who were seen as potentially threatening. Bigwood, for example, talked about his initial impression of being locked up. "Going there scared me outta my wits," he recalled. "I thought, 'This is the real deal. Locked in a cell.'" He was filled with feelings of remorse. "I thought about my mom and what shame she must be feeling," but realized that expressing fearful emotions was taboo. He viewed the regs with awe and respect. "These guys were gangsters. These guys got something. They're tough. They're getting tattoos." His later interpretations of himself, as he made the transition from juvenile to adult institutions and began using heroin, indicate that he was still fearful about being incarcerated and did not yet see himself as a reg. "I was intimidated when I first got there." However, he soon became accepted and educated by others, mostly heroin addicts, about the norms and values of this peculiar social world:

> I got taken under the wing by some guy that had been down [incarcerated] off and on for all his life basically and he was like 20 years older than me. And he and his partners schooled me about doin' time, racism, the whole deal.

In short, he was learning new values through his associations and interactions with others who were already a part of this deviant world (Sutherland, 1939). After his first release from an adult facility, his developing self-concept as a reg was firming up nicely. Successful completion of a prison term was evidence that he was "bad." "I got out and I was, ah, I'm really tough now." By then, he found himself immersed within a social world that had heroin use and the code of the streets at its core.

Although the wannabes had difficulty adapting to the routine of doing time inside penal institutions, it could have been worse. They were aided by their prior acquaintance with meanings and values of the street that they had learned from their associations with regulars. Once locked up, they discovered that the same norms existed behind bars. Doctor Dee told me that he was first locked up as an adult. His initial trip behind bars was in the Los Angeles County Jail. It was "pretty terrifying" at first, he said. But his association with people previously who had done time made it easier for him. His familiarity with them and the stories he had heard about being locked up helped him know what to expect and eased the difficulty of the transition. He quickly found that the same guys he looked up to in the outside world were doing well in jail. They became his mentors. "That's where I got introduced to the term 'reg,'" he recalled.

"And that's what I aspired to be. They were the ones who showed me the ropes." To be like a reg, he began doing things the way they did. He learned about ironing his clothes jailhouse style. "I learned how to press my jailhouse clothes with a scrub brush and put 'em under the mattress to dry." He learned how to heat coffee water by lighting compressed toilet paper with a match and holding it under a metal cup. In short, he learned a behavioral style that made doing time easier. "As time progressed I learned all the ropes. That place became like my home. And, over time, I became a reg."

Prison was not a place where wannabes learned crime, as some opponents of prison claim. Rather, it was a finishing school in which they perfected their performances as regulars. The fruit of their pursuits was acceptance by a group of people they admired and an ability to decently survive while in custody. For wannabes, becoming a reg entailed a change in the way they saw themselves. This, in turn, affected the way they saw others, the world, and their behavior for years to come.

DRIFTERS[5]

The common feature of the final nine fellas was that they came from middle-class backgrounds and, during their young lives, had more of a tendency to "drift" between conventional and deviant activities than did the wannabes and regulars. Further, the drifters typically embraced several identities when they were young.

The concept of drift can be understood as a gradual process of movement in which a youngster, affected by a variety of underlying influences, takes actions that are defined as deviant according to mainstream norms. For drift to take place, an individual must be loosened, at least temporarily, from conventional means of social control and, at the same time, have the inclination and opportunity to take part in illegal activities common to some adolescent subculture (Matza, 1964). When confronted by figures of authority, the young drifters often used techniques of neutralization to rationalize their behavior (Sykes and Matza, 1957). Unlike the regs, the deviant groups they associated with were not typically characterized by the values of the street. Unlike the wannabes, they did not necessarily aspire to be like regs. Like others who have been defined as drifters, they were representative of a majority of young males who get involved with petty criminal activity during their youth but do not grow up to become adult criminals (Matza, 1964; Moffitt, 1993).

Who They Were

Bozo was a 50-year-old African American who had six months clean at the time of the interviews. Altogether, he had done about three years in jails and prisons. I met Bozo in an NA meeting. He always had a positive attitude that

---

[5] The concept comes from David Matza's *Delinquency and Drift* (1964).

seemed to brighten up the room whenever he spoke. Well educated, he had moved to California from New York to leave behind his heroin using lifestyle and start a new life. As I interviewed him, I was struck by his passion, humor, and sense of empathy toward other recovering addicts.

Winky had done a total of five years in prison, had 16 years clean, and was 53 years old when we met for the interview. A powerful role model for other recovering people in his community, Winky often went out of his way to lend a caring hand to others. When I initially called him to request an interview, he asked me to meet him at a certain address on a Wednesday evening. From there, we would figure out a time and location to talk. He told me someone he knew from AA was dying and a group of people were gathering at his house because he was no longer able to attend meetings elsewhere. So I, who would never have been doing this if I had not been seeking an interview, went and participated in the meeting. Winky was there—so were about 10 others. In the center of the small living room lay a huge man who, suffering from cancer, was near death. He could no longer walk, roll over, go to the bathroom by himself, or eat. As I sat there that evening, I was humbled and moved to hear what people in the room had to say about their feelings, fears, and ideas about their dying friend. Often in tears, they spoke about how awkward it was to be there because they were uncomfortable in the presence of someone they loved who was dying. As the meeting unfolded, Winky massaged the man's body, whispered in his ear, and showed him love and support like I have seldom seen. And when the dying man spoke, the words he uttered were perhaps the most honest I have ever heard. Unashamedly, he shared his fear. Openly weeping, he expressed how grateful he was to have people who loved him in the room. By the time I left, Winky and I made an agreement about a time and place to meet. As I went on my way, I was overcome with the feeling that some of these ex-convicts I was interviewing were far removed from the stereotypical image of a criminal dope fiend.

Wino was a white, 46-year-old who had managed to stay clean for 2 years. Overall, he had done about 12 years in jails and prisons in two different states. Wino was one of the fellas I was introduced to by someone I had known in NA. We got together at his home for the interview on an early summer evening. Our encounter was somewhat awkward because, for one thing, we were relative strangers when we met. His quiet, shy disposition also seemed to inhibit his ability to open up. Like a few of the other fellas, he often struggled to find anything to say. Overall, though, his contribution was very helpful.

Hippie was a white, 50-year-old who had spent three years in prison in his early twenties. He had been clean eight years when we met for the interview. I first got to know Hippie by attending NA meetings. Unlike many of the other fellas, he had spent most of his adult life outside of penal institutions. After going to prison when he was younger, he managed to develop stakes in the mainstream culture and stay out for good. However, he used heroin until his life became so horrible that he sought help in a drug program where he began to look at himself and start the process of recovery. Reflective of his intelligence, his story proved to be especially insightful.

Bird was a white, 49-year-old who, after spending 7 years behind bars, had been clean for 12 years. I did not know Bird before the interview. In fact, I only met with him once in person. He was working as a counselor in an out-patient drug, alcohol, and HIV program at the time, which is where we got together. Like me, Bird enjoyed surfing and blues music. These two common interests, our similar backgrounds, and his ability to be articulate in telling of his life history resulted in what seemed to be a pleasant, fruitful encounter for us both.

Brains was a white, 42-year-old who had been locked up for roughly 11 years. At the time we met, he had 4 months clean. Like Huero, Baggy, and Kickstand (who he had known since they were kids), he was also living at Hope House. Brains seemed to have a photographic memory. He could recall things, especially when it came to anything related to music, as if he had a built-in computer in his head. He appeared to be a quiet, intelligent, caring type of guy who was doing his best to make it in the outside world as a clean, recovering addict.

Rabbit was a close friend. Our relationship began in the mid-1980s in one of those old, gray-walled penitentiaries built around 1840. As we each got "short," which means soon to be released from custody (usually 2 to 3 years), we were sent to a forest camp outside the walls. In contrast to the bleak environment of the prison, the wall-less, fence-less, camp-without-gun-towers was located in a beautiful coastal mountain range in the Pacific Northwest. There, our friendship blossomed. We worked on the same crew felling trees with chain saws, fighting fires, planting trees, and making the big bucks—which came to something like $3.00 a day. Some of the experiences we shared during that period were highlights of my life. Interestingly, the interview with Rabbit took place on a mountainside near Lake Tahoe several years after each of us had been released. At that time he had spent a total of 14 years in jails and prisons, had almost 2 years clean, and was 49 years old.

Shasta was a 45-year-old Chicano. Altogether he had been incarcerated for 10 years, more or less. He had 5 years clean when we met for the interview. I met Shasta in NA meetings. As with several of the other fellas, our past experiences with the California prison system and street-oriented, heroin-addict lifestyles brought us together like two ex-army guys who form an immediate bond after discovering they both fought in the same war. Before and after the many meetings we both attended over the years, we often got together for a few minutes and talked, usually with gratitude and humor, about how far removed we were from our old ways of living.

Vardo was a white, 42-year-old who had spent roughly six years behind bars. He became a close friend of mine throughout the 1990s, and had eight years clean at the time of the interview. Before getting clean, he and Doctor Dee had known each other for several years. In fact, Vardo, who got clean first, was instrumental in Doctor Dee's initial entrance into the world of recovery. Like Bird and me, Vardo enjoyed surfing and blues music. As well as attending 12-step meetings, he worked in the field of drug and alcohol treatment.

Where They Came From

The drifters tended to follow socially accepted, middle-class routes into adulthood. They tended to play sports and do odd jobs such as mowing lawns or delivering papers in their neighborhoods to earn spending money. School attendance was seldom a serious problem. Most finished high school and some went to college. Others began working regularly, and some went into the armed services. The mainstream paths they took, however, were diverted towards deviant directions.

Violence in their homes was one factor that may have altered the drifters' paths. Several talked about getting regularly whipped by their parents or siblings. Winky talked a little about what it was like when he was a kid in southern California in the 1950s. His parents performed middle-class roles common to that era. "Dad worked in an aircraft factory as a manager. Mom was a housewife." The family was economically sound. "We had a couple cars in the driveway and a three bedroom house on an acre lot in the San Fernando Valley," he recalled. Yet, physical violence because of tension between family members was common within the household:

> Inside there was a lotta violence going on. At some point my brother turned mean on me and he started whopping me regular. Dad'd come home and Mom'd say the boys did this or that and his best answer was to whip on us, or whip on my brother for whipping on me.

Getting beaten drove an emotional wedge between himself and his family.

Though the reasons varied, several of the drifters claimed to feel different and unappreciated as youngsters. Bird, who grew up in a middle-class environment, talked about feeling alienated and unpleasantly unique as a child because he never knew his father. Moreover, his name was altered after he was adopted at age six. In his mind, most other kids knew their dads and kept the same names:

> It was confusing. I always saw myself as completely different than everybody else. None of the other kids I went to school with were going to court having their names changed. So, from the beginning I felt different than the rest of them.

He claimed to be further affected by the disapproving manner in which he was dealt with by his stepfather. Bird said, "It was just the way he treated me. He never did like me. The opinion I got from him was I wasn't worthy of a conversation, the time of day, any of that. Just keep your mouth shut and we'll feed you." His family issues were compounded by health problems. He used to have to take medication because he had epileptic seizures as a kid. Again, he felt different. "I have seizures and nobody else I know has seizures." After having a seizure in the second grade, he started getting treated as an outsider. For instance, kids wouldn't pick him to play on a team in the schoolyard. "I wasn't as good as the rest of them. That was the impression I got."

A few of the drifters indicated that their childhoods were without trauma. They did not complain about getting whipped or feeling different or unappreciated. They were happy with their home lives, friends, and schools. Bozo, for example, talked about growing up in a neighborhood in New York City. He said he came from a good family who cared about him, went to a "typical" school, and, in general, saw himself as a normal person. He recalled, "I didn't see myself as abnormal. I saw myself as an average person. We were average kids growing up in the mid '60s." He did say that as a black kid, he was exposed to prejudice early in his life. He also recognized that there were economic and social differences between blacks and whites. He told me, "It didn't trigger that much anger 'cause I was more or less content with what I had. My parents took care of me." These drifters, compared with the others, did not seem to feel especially alienated by anything they experienced as youngsters. Their experiences and the way they were interpreted appear to have helped these fellas develop fairly positive self-evaluations and outlooks on life.

Early Drug Use

Several drifters were attracted to illegal drug use because it was taboo and, therefore exciting. Others began "using" because of their exposure to drugs and a willingness to try something new. A minority felt it was necessary to get high to avoid being excluded from certain groups. All of them had used other drugs or alcohol before they tried heroin. Though the majority began getting high in their teenage years, two began drinking alcohol while they were in grade school.

For drifters, the preexisting condition making it possible to drift into social worlds that included heroin use was prior affiliation with some type of group that participated in deviant, often illegal activities. Bozo, for example, said that he began using the drug after returning from the Vietnam War. Before getting drafted, he used to "party"—drink alcohol, smoke "reefer" (marijuana) and have a good time. He continued partying while overseas. Once he got back to the states, he began attending college in Michigan. During a visit to his hometown in New York, he looked up an old friend who informed him that things had changed since he left. He was told that instead of weed and wine, heroin was now the thing to do and that, as some was displayed, "this is the shit right here." Not wanting to be left out, he tried it. "The real decision to do it had to do with the idea that this is what everyone else was doing." The process of neutralization affected his drift into heroin use. Neutralization techniques, as suggested by Gresham Sykes and David Matza (1957), are means one uses to maintain a good image about oneself while doing deviant things. In this case, Bozo blamed his drug use on others. He used heroin, he said, "because everyone else was doing it." This explanation helped him escape self-defamation.

Over time, Bozo developed a taste for the narcotic. At first, he snorted it. Before long, he was fixing. Soon he found himself drifting between conventional and deviant social worlds to keep himself supplied with the drug. He recalled, "I ended up having to leave my school environment and go to the ghettos of Detroit to hook up with people I didn't even know. I had to find them so I could find my dope." His yearning for heroin and the actions he had to take to use it proved difficult:

> It was hard to go to college and use. I lived off campus and once I found out where that dope was I was out there a lot. It was like being in two different worlds. I'd get high at night, go to school from 8 to 3, plus I had a job on campus. I also had a GI bill grant.

The inconsistency in the way he saw himself likely left him with a sense of inner turmoil and confusion. In the ghettos, he was an addict. At school, he was a college student. "I lived life from day to day. Like, okay, I got this major. I'd go from this major to that. But then I'd get out of school and go get high. So I didn't know who the fuck I was," he said. After seeing himself as an "average kid growing up in the '60s," a Vietnam vet, and a college student, he gradually became a criminally oriented addict. He recalled that as his need for the drug increased so did its price. "The two dollar bags turned to dime [ten dollar] bags." He began doing forgery-related crimes to get money. It seemed as if the purpose of his life had changed. Now it was all about heroin. "There were no more parties. There was no more fun. Once I got into that heroin I didn't wanna do nothing else." Things he valued because of his ties to the mainstream culture started falling away. "My lifestyle changed. I didn't care about things anymore. My GPA went down." Bozo's story is illustrative of drifters who began using the drug because of what is popularly called peer pressure. They tried heroin to feel included within a group they admired, usually made up of people in the early stages of experimentation with the drug. Individuals who had been using it for years and had been to prison were not typically a part of the circle.

For some drifters, further pursuit of heroin had more to do with its effects than with any need to attain status or inclusion within a deviant group. However, use of the drug eventually pulled all of them into deviant lifestyles. Brains talked about the lack of deviance associated with his early heroin career, which began when he was 14 years old. He explained, "I came from a very good, loving family. Neither my father or mother used alcohol or drugs of any kind. Did well in school. Graduated a year early out of high school. Good grades." His introduction to heroin came about when he agreed to accompany his next-door neighbor, an older friend, to a house where the drug was being used. Though he knew several people there, they were not his only associations. "It was just this one circle of friends." He more commonly hung out with kids who were involved with athletics. His earliest impression of heroin was extremely positive. "I remember doing it and it was an instant love affair. That's all I can say." Brains drifted into an alien social world where the opportunity to use heroin presented itself. Once he tried it, he found that it brought him great pleasure.

Unlike regulars and wannabes, the drifters were typically attracted toward groups that were not associated with convicts and violence, but several were drawn toward illegal drugs because of the drugs' forbidden, taboo status. As are many young males, they were somewhat rebellious and attracted towards deviant activities (Matza, 1964). For them, drug use symbolized a lack of conformity to mainstream standards, a way of being different, a means of identifying with deviant groups and a way to have fun. Winky proved to be a good example. He associated his initial attraction to marijuana with its illegal status. "I liked smoking weed because it was against the law. In those days you could go do serious time for pot. So that was cool." Further, he admired certain deviant groups who used these drugs and did his best to emulate them:

> Being a head, beatniks, jazz musicians—that's who did that. I wanted to be like those guys. And I adopted that as my identity. If you thought of me you thought of me as a head.[6] Started out smoking pot—that became who I was.

Winky's aspirations were affected by the meanings given to deviant groups who used drugs in the 1950s and early 1960s. His admiration of the "heads" was similar to how the wannabes perceived the regulars in that he noticed a deviant group outside himself with which he hoped to identify. The allure of illegal drugs for several of the drifters, then, was greatly associated with the symbolic meaning of participating in taboo activities. In addition, it was a means of identifying with deviant groups. But instead of aspiring to become regulars, they tended to admire and emulate nonviolent groups such as beatniks, heads, and hippies.

Drug use, however, had a lot to do with their self-evaluations once they started getting high. Different self-concepts, in fact, often became associated with specific drugs. Hippie's early life provides a good example. His parents drank alcohol. They were his role models "and their role models were drinkers, like Frank Sinatra and Dino Martin. That whole era of people—I mean booze was the lubricant. Everybody drank." For him, drinking alcohol was a symbol of growing up. He told me, "I wanted to be an adult. Didn't wanna be a kid. So I started drinking when I was 12." As the years passed and he made it to high school, he became involved in several types of roles and activities, drifting from one to the next. He tried surfing and "took on the surfer look for awhile." Then he smoked marijuana and became attracted to a group known as the greasers who rode in cars that were low to the ground and wore greased back hair. "I saw myself at that point as not really a greaser but on the fringes of that crowd." His infatuation with the greasers, who were probably like regulars, was short-lived. Next, he identified himself with jazz music lovers and their unique characteristics. "So then I started to see myself as a bohemian beatnik." By 1966, he smoked pot and drank alcohol regularly. One night at a drive-in movie, he took some LSD. The effects of the drug had a powerful impact:

> It pretty much changed everything about me. I didn't drink for two years after that. Then it was just dope. That psychedelic experience created a

---

[6] A "head" was a slang term used to define someone known to use illegal drugs in the 1950s and 1960s. Generally, heads did not participate in serious criminal activity as did heroin addicts and were not as likely to spend time in prison.

big shift in how I perceived the world and, I reckon, in how I perceived myself. I mean I got a sense of my self as a spiritual being. It just expanded my consciousness big time.

Hippie was also greatly affected by the countercultural movement that was beginning to take off across the country:

At the same time all that stuff was just starting to happen—that consciousness expanding, dope smoking, flower power, hippie, love, peace—and the Vietnam war was just starting to crank up but nobody knew about it yet.

He remembered reading an article in *Ramparts* magazine that discussed all the reasons why the United States had no place in Vietnam. The negative effect it had on his ideas about the conflict had a further impact on the way he saw himself:

I always figured I'd go in the service. Everybody goes in the army. But after I read that article I knew I never would. Now I saw myself as some- one who was a draft dodger-conscientious objector. There was no way I was going to fight in that war.

His thinking was affected by social forces that were common to thousands of others who were becoming part of the counterculture during this period. As his anti-establishment perspective took root, his exposure to and involvement with illegal activities, most of which were related to drugs, increased. After an arrest for being in a place where marijuana was being smoked and losing his job at a telephone company because he would not cut his hair, he began selling illegal drugs. "I just started dealing grass. Weed, hash, acid too now and then." He seldom did opiates. Actually, he had an aversion toward people who used heroin. "I had a prejudice against junkies. I saw myself as better than that, as a hippie." Hippie clearly wore several "hats" when he was young. For awhile, he was a middle-class kid who drank. Then he emulated surfers, greasers, beat- niks, and jazz musicians. Finally, he developed the perspective of a hippie.

Some drifters began getting high because it felt good. Some did it because it was "what everyone else was doing." Others began because they were curi- ous, rebellious, and attracted to its taboo qualities. Drug use provided them with a way to be different, a means of identification, and was seen as a "cool" thing to do. Regardless of their reasons for starting, they were all headed in a similar direction.

Early Incarceration

As youngsters, the drifters were not surrounded by friends, relatives, and ac- quaintances who went to prison. Compared with the regs, and to a lesser ex- tent the wannabes, the effects, meanings, and ways of being associated with the social worlds that flourish in places of forced confinement were basically unfamiliar. When they first were incarcerated, they were greeted by what they perceived to be a hostile, oppressive, frightening social world.

Vardo's story provides a good representation of the general way the drifters perceived their first trip behind bars. At the time of his first arrest, he was an 18-year-old surfer who liked to get high. He came from a middle-class, white suburb south of Los Angeles. Though he had dabbled with opiates, he had never been addicted. As it happened, he was first confined in the Los Angeles County jail. From beginning to end, the episode was filled with fear. "I was scared to death," he recalled. Part of his fear had to do with being around large numbers of racial minorities and guards who seemed to do everything within their power to degrade prisoners:

> I'd been around blacks and Mexicans, but not that much. So now I'm scared. I don't know what's happening. These are not like the surfer guys I'd been around. Now I'm having to mix with all these different kinds of people. And the cops are just fucked, you know. They're just demoralizing you.

Degrading prisoners or degradation ceremonies (Garfinkel, 1956) are a means of social control used by agents of authority to belittle individuals and influence their future behavior. In the military, these tactics are used to make new recruits see themselves as part of the same unit. In jail and prison, they have the same effect, except the "unit" they are exposed to happens to be the violent social world of the regulars. These ceremonies help create a state of drift and increase the likelihood that prisoners will take on the values and meanings of the penitentiary or the street.

Tactics of degradation included name calling by guards and warnings about the dangers that awaited them in the jail. Vardo recalled, "They're calling you a piece of shit. Telling you you're gonna get fucked in here. You're gonna get beat up. So you're getting more afraid." Vardo compared getting processed into LA County jail to what he imagined it was like entering a German concentration camp as a captive during World War II:

> I've never been to Auschwitz, but its gotta be as fucked, because there's so many people, and you go in phases, like cows. And everyone is stuffed into these little fuckin holding cells. Tempers are short fused. People are fucked up and cut up. You go from room to room.

Every prisoner was eventually led to a Plexiglas-covered window where he would provide background information such as his place of birth, age, and health problems to a guard. Time dragged and the process was slow. One of the most humiliating and frightening experiences he recalled was the strip search. He claimed that the guards, who always addressed prisoners with contempt, lined him up with about 60 others and ordered everyone to get naked. While the men undressed, they were yelled at constantly:

> Now we've got 10 cops walking in front of us like fucking drill sergeants. Talking shit like, "Fucking nigger, get your feet back on that fucking line"—screaming. They're just humiliating everyone. Some old man that can't even get undressed—they're yelling at him—"Fucking old man. Hurry up you piece of shit. What're you doing here anyway?"

His level of fear escalated as the degradation ceremony continued. At one point, he remembered the guards pulled a guy out of the line and slammed his body against a concrete wall for not obeying their orders. Their violent actions and screaming voices made him want to do all he could to comply with their wishes. "You don't wanna fuck up 'cause you think they'll kill you." He recalled the foul smell of the place as the clothes began being peeled away from the men in the line. "It stunk like human garbage. 'Cause everyone's fucked up. Smells like throw up. People have been throwing up. Smells like shit 'cause there's a bunch of people shitting and pissing in the same place." After about an hour of standing around naked following the strip search, he was given a chance to quickly shower in freezing cold water, sprayed with insecticide by guards, and given his jailhouse clothes and bedroll. Finally, after two days of being processed, he made it to a cell where, because of overcrowded conditions, he had to sleep underneath a bunk on the concrete floor with only a blanket for a mattress. After a day or two, he got his own bunk, which made things a little better. Yet, he remained scared during his entire stay. His fear was enhanced by the way he interpreted his surroundings and by sounds he had never before heard:

> I'm scared all the time. That's all I remember. I was afraid like all the time. Because it was like hell. At night it was like being in the caverns of hell. You could hear screams. You could hear rattling fucking bars and people saying, "Let me outta here." And you hear fights. Dice rolling. Shit like you've never heard before. Cries. I heard cries like I never heard before. Like death cries. Like people just getting fucked or beat or something.

He dreaded when it was time to eat because that meant leaving the cell and being around other prisoners who would wait on the freeway[7] to walk to the chow hall. On one occasion, he was confronted and attacked by a large, black prisoner. "He hit me really hard—cut my face—blackened my eye." Now he was really scared. He ended up doing nearly 90 days in the county jail that time. His charge was "being in a place where marijuana was being smoked."

The narratives of the early drifter experiences behind bars can be seen as evidence that they had different self-concepts and perspectives than the regulars and wannabes. Unlike the regs, they did not shine while in custody. They did not see jail as a place where they were a "success" or "king of the castle." As they aged and continued to use heroin, they would become more accustomed to penal institutions. In general, what may at one time have seemed like "the caverns of hell," came to be perceived as normal.

---

[7] In LA County Jail, the freeway is what otherwise might be called a tier or walkway. It is the space between the front of the cells and an adjoining cement wall—an area of about three feet. The freeway is as long as the cellblock, but it is so narrow that there is barely enough space to accommodate the large numbers of prisoners who spend considerable time waiting to walk to other areas of the jail where they might eat, receive visits, or wait for court.

Table 3.1 Fellas at the Time of the Interviews

W-White; C-Chicano; M-Mexican; B-Black

Name	Race	Age	Time "in"	Clean time
Regulars				
Huero	W	46	15 years	35 days
Baggy	C	46	5 years	8 months
Pelon	C	47	18 years	7 years
Jumbo	C	58	7 years	6 years
Wheels	W	46	15 years	11 years
Sticks	B	49	19 years	4 years
Weasel	M	61	12 years	8 years
Kickstand	W	46	25 years	90 days
Wannabes				
Junior	C	52	7 years	12 years
Bigwood	W	42	8 years	13 months
Doctor Dee	W	44	9.5 years	5 years
Drifters				
Bozo	B	50	3 years	6 months
Winky	W	53	5 years	16 years
Wino	W	46	12 years	2 years
Hippie	W	50	3 years	8 years
Bird	W	49	7 years	12 years
Brains	W	42	11 years	4 months
Rabbit	W	49	14 years	2 years
Shasta	C	49	10 years	5 years
Vardo	W	42	6 years	8 years

SUMMARY

The regulars in this study came from mostly lower socioeconomic environments in which violence, doing time in prison and the use of illegal drugs were the norm. As youngsters, they were inclined to feel out of place or inferior when they had to spend time around people they saw as different than themselves (e.g., people in the school environment). Disobeying rules, using illegal drugs, fighting, and, in general, being "tough" were ways of dealing with their feelings of alienation and inferiority. For regs, being "bad" as defined by mainstream standards was seen as good. Without exception, they all had histories of juvenile incarceration. In these facilities, and in the adult institutions that would follow, they were seen and treated with respect by others like themselves.

The wannabes aspired to be like regulars. Their early motivations to use illegal drugs, especially heroin, had more to do with their desires to fit in with the regs than anything else. In short, the wannabes perceived the lifestyles and characteristics of the regulars to be enticing and tried to emulate them.

The drifters came from middle-class backgrounds. Most had no juvenile record. Their early drug use came about because they were curious and rebellious. Some began using heroin because it was available and the effects brought great pleasure. Others were initially attracted to illegal drugs in general because of their taboo status. As youth, they "drifted" between conventional and deviant activities more than did the members of the other groups and had the most difficulty adapting to worlds of imprisonment. To varying degrees, the processes associated with prisonization, which are the focus of the next chapter, pushed them toward identifying as regulars.

4

Going Deeper:
Prisonization

After entering the world of heroin addiction, I began noticing differences among the addicts who passed through my life. At one end of the spectrum were those that presented images of themselves that reflected their association with the street. These individuals, often regulars, had usually spent time behind bars. To make money, they typically engaged in different forms of "junkie work," or "hustles" (Biernacki, 1979), which included petty thefts, prostitution, burglaries, dope dealing, and so on to support their daily habits. At the other end were those who were far removed from the lifestyles and values of the street. These types, sometimes called "chippers" (Crawford et al., 1983, 701), generally worked at regular jobs and got high only occasionally—like on weekends after being paid—and seldom participated in any type of illegal activity other than the simple use of the drug. It is unlikely that anyone spending even a brief amount of time with some chippers and regulars would fail to notice their dramatic differences. The appearance and style of the street, which one group has and the other does not, is difficult to overlook.

Of importance here are the ways I saw these various types changing over time. The street addicts often disappeared because they would get arrested or killed during violent confrontations. Some that went to prison would return after their sentences were finished. Others never got out or died inside. I saw many switch from heroin to cheap red wine as they aged. In contrast to street addicts, whose self-concepts and behavior seemed to change very little, I witnessed several chippers undergo what seemed like a total metamorphosis. They would go from being regularly employed, generally law-abiding, occasional users to full-blown street addicts. In most of these cases, this process was greatly affected by periods of incarceration.

The story of a friend represents the radical transformation of identity that many non–street-oriented drug users go through by spending time behind bars. Max was a guy in his late twenties that I got to know while attending college. Years before this, he had spent a short amount of time in custody as a juvenile. When we met, he appeared to be a relatively well-adjusted citizen. As well as living with Sandy, the mother of his two-year-old daughter, he was a skilled, employed auto mechanic. Max ended up dabbling with heroin. At first, he was getting high only occasionally. Within a few months, though, he was using it daily and became addicted. Because of the shame and stigma associated with using the drug, he kept what he was doing secret. Eventually, his money supply dried up and his level of desperation to acquire more escalated. Before long, he was caught forging checks and sent to prison. Because of his juvenile conviction, he was sentenced under California's "three strikes you're out" law and had to serve just over four years. This, his second strike, meant that any future felony conviction will result in a sentence of 25 years to life. During his incarceration, we corresponded by mail. By merely reading his letters, I noticed he was changing. I saw him only once after he paroled. He was like a different person. His self-concept, language, demeanor, and overall perspective had undergone a severe alteration. Not only was his body covered with tattoos, but his ideas, plans, and hopes for the future were extremely different than the ones he seemed to have when we first met. The last I heard about him, he was still "out" (not locked up) and battling with his drug habit. His name had also changed. Nowadays, instead of being called Max, he goes by the name Mad Dog, a nickname he picked up in prison.

The change in Max illustrates the effects of prisonization, which is the focus of this chapter. Like immigrants to the United States becoming "Americanized," prisonization is equated with assimilation into the social world of the prison. The consequences of this process will vary and be influenced by pre-prison experiences and affiliation with groups, often-deviant subcultures (for example, drug addicts, gang membership), in the outside world (Irwin and Cressey, 1962; Irwin, 1970). The degree to which one is prisonized will have some influence on how well he fares while he is doing time, and what he does after being released.

It is important to note that the social structure of the prison is always changing. This, in turn affects the process of prisonization and the outlooks of convicts. During the first half of the 20th century, prisoners developed a relatively cohesive social system that served them and their keepers well. Among other things, it gave them a means of rejecting their rejecters rather than themselves (McKorkle and Korn, 1954). Within this world was found a distinct social hierarchy, unique patterns of speech, and a variety of social roles. Convicts ran the prison, kept the peace, did almost all the work, and were seldom bothered by prison administrators. Of great importance was the powerful value system, the convict code, which gave prisoners a sense of self-respect and dignity (Austin and Irwin, 2001, 90–91; Irwin, 1970, 1980). It allowed them to neutralize the implications of their situation and develop self-conceptions as good and decent individuals (Sykes and Matza, 1957). At the heart of this code were specific, unwritten rules of conduct that included minding your own business, playing it cool, never informing on another convict, never breaking your word, never showing weakness, and communicating with guards as little as possible. Adhering to these values allowed one to be seen not only as a person with integrity, but as a convict rather than an inmate, which was a derogatory label.

Though it was gradually fading, this cohesive prisoner system was still in place to some degree while I was doing time in California in the mid-1970s. The convict code still had meaning, but mostly within the context of certain smaller groups rather than the population as a whole. Racist tension was always high. When violence occurred it was usually extreme. When it was not occurring, it was a constant threat. Gangs did exist, but most of us were not affiliated directly and hung out together because we were from the same race and geographic area. It was here I first heard the word "homeboy," a term people called each other when they came from the same neighborhood or county. Convicts, those at the top of the prisoner hierarchy, were treated with respect and greatly influenced the running of the institution. They were usually the ones holding key positions of power. The "assignment clerk" was the guy you went to see if you wanted a job. The fee was usually two cartons of cigarettes. The "dental clerk" could get you into the dentist right away, for a price.

During my first commitment, because I made the right convict contacts and knew how to read and type, I was able to land a clerk job in the "Receiving and Release" (R & R) office shortly after my arrival. This position gave me access to information about who would be arriving in the institution the day before they arrived. One of the things I was expected to do, a tradition that had been in place for years (and was taught to me by the man I replaced), included making three lists of these soon-to-be-new prisoners before they arrived. On each list, which the guards could never see, I put their names, race, county of origin, and crime. Once completed, I gave a copy to a black, brown, and white prisoner (racial lines were crossed in certain circumstances). In return, I was rewarded with something tangible, such as cigarettes or a small amount of marijuana, and social status. This process served the purpose of screening incoming prisoners. Each race was responsible for determining who could stay, or who had to go. If, for instance, a white prisoner with a reputation as an informant was to arrive the next day, it was the responsibility of the whites to make sure he did not remain in the mainline population. Such a person would be either physically assaulted or encouraged to seek protective custody from prison officials.

Today, largely because of the conservative get-tough-on-crime rhetoric outlined in Chapter 2, harsher drug laws, and the changing racial composition of penal institutions in the last half of the 20th century, the old social system of the prison is little more than a remnant from the past. In 1923, for example, 31 percent of prisoners were black. By 1997, 49 percent were black and 18 percent came from Hispanic backgrounds. This racial skewing stems from the fact that the majority of present-day prisoners come from America's mostly nonwhite inner-cities where people still live only because of their lower-classed, economic circumstances and their inability to flee to the suburbs. Here, young, undereducated males are raised amidst deplorable social conditions that include extremely limited opportunities and unemployment rates that reach as high as 50 percent. To bide their time and generate incomes, many of these youngsters become immersed in the culture of the street and often become involved in illegal activities, such as selling drugs. Demonized by the mainstream culture, they make easy targets for police and are increasingly arrested and incarcerated (Austin and Irwin, 2001, 94–95).

Racial hostility, often encouraged by prison officials as a means of control, was (and is) a major component of America's prisons (Bacon et al., 1971, 110; Wood, 1997). As in the wider society, racial conflicts escalated in the 1960s when nonwhite populations began to assert themselves, often violently, in prison affairs (Austin and Irwin, 2001, 95). Always more severe in higher security institutions, these tensions led to the development of gangs and cliques, increased violence, de facto segregation of prisoner social life, and the gradual collapse of the old prison culture, which has largely been replaced by the meanings and values of the inner-cities. A prisoner I met while I was doing time, currently housed in a maximum security federal prison, recently responded to a letter I sent him about what I mistakenly believed were the similarities between the convict code and Anderson's (1999) code of the streets. His words brilliantly outline the basis and effects of the evolving behavioral "codes" inside prisons:

> The inner city mores have saturated and become the prevailing "code" in maximum security settings—to the point that they override any and all preexisting prison values systems. It's obvious why. The drug laws have inundated these places with a disproportionate number of young inner-city kids serving sentences many of them will be unable to complete.
>
> The so-called "code of the streets" bears no resemblance whatsoever to the pre-historic convict code you and I grew up with. These kids are quick to inform—either for personal gain (be it material or favoritism from their keepers), fear, or spite.
>
> The different street gangs are constantly involved in a dynamic where they are jockeying for a favored position that facilitates their particular power agenda. Put simply, they inform, they exploit the weak, they create loud grandstanding situations that bring everyone's, including the man's, attention to their disagreements. And they prey on all but those whom their instincts tell them are more serious predators—old school convicts like myself who aren't going to posture or "fake" as they call it, but instead will respond to an incursion upon my personal space with an immediate, ruthlessly efficient attempt to seriously injure or kill them.
>
> The convict is fast becoming an extinct entity. The few of us that remain are quite cynical about the state of prisons today, and filled with distrust. To a large degree, the old ways of resistance are no more. Now it

seems as if the primary goal of virtually every person you take the time to observe is to feather his own nest at any cost. Integrity? Sense of honor? Keeping one's word? For the most part, out the window.

Despite these changes, much of prison life remains an extension of the past. Backing down from confrontation continues to be seen as weak and unacceptable. Seasoned prisoners still use laughter to help maintain their convict identities. As well as downplay their dreadful situations, humor helps them distinguish moral and social boundaries, express pain and masculinity, and constantly denigrate the various aspects of the criminal justice system (Terry, 1997).

Rather than being generally cohesive, however, prison societies have become increasingly fragmented. Gang affiliation and violence have escalated. Loyalty to other prisoners has declined. John Irwin, a well respected criminologist who once was also a prisoner, explained two decades ago that

> [t]he respected public prison figure—the convict or hog—stands ready to kill to protect himself [and] maintains strong loyalties to some small group of other convicts (invariably of his own race). He openly and stubbornly opposes the administration, even if this results in harsh punishment. (Irwin, 1980, 195)

Based on what I witnessed during my own days behind bars in the 1980s, as well as information gathered from people who have been doing time since my last release, I believe it is safe to say that Irwin's words are as applicable today as they were when first written.

The demise of prisoner cohesion has made the process of prisonization even more damaging than in the past. Where before most prisoners were able to maintain positive self-evaluations because of the ethics they fulfilled as mandated by the convict code, now they often withdraw from most prison public activities and disassociate themselves from the convict identity. In their quest for safety and, perhaps, some semblance of sanity, they are left with little or no supportive countervalues whatsoever. These were the guys I would see who, in increasing numbers over the years, seldom left their cells and never went to the yard. Now held in contempt by both the prison authorities and other prisoners, they are left completely alienated and become almost incapable of making a successful transition to the outside world after release (Austin and Irwin, 2001, 112).

Every society is characterized by a unique set of norms and values that not everyone is able to fulfill. Those who obey the cultural rules feel morally superior to those who violate them (Durkheim, [1893] 1964). Prison is no different. There, deviants are those who do not live by the prevailing code of ethics. Living outside the cultural norms of the prison leaves them vulnerable to attacks and criticisms. Nobody is exempt from the effects of these codes. Irwin explains that those

> who consciously attempt to pass through the prison experience without acquiring any convict beliefs and values do to some extent acquire certain meanings, certain taken-for-granted interpretations and responses to

situations which will shape, influence, or distort reality for them after release. (Irwin, 1970, 83)

It was this changing social world the fellas stepped into, some all the way back in the 1960s. Listening to them talk about themselves within the context of their prison experiences provides insight into how the cultural mores and values of that world are transmitted. Though the code of the streets may be the prevailing norm of prison today, the old convict code still had great meaning among the fellas at the time of the interviews and will therefore be used extensively in the telling of their stories.

THE FELLAS' THOUGHTS
ON BEING CONVICTS

There was a notable difference regarding the way the men talked about convicts compared with other prisoners during the interviews. All the fellas were familiar with the basic ideals of prison that hold that cooperating with authorities, being convicted of sex crimes, and backing down from confrontations are taboo. The idea that convicts have status and are worthy of respect still meant a lot, especially for the regs who talked about them in a positive light. Jumbo, for example, said he viewed convicts as being smart and trustworthy. "Very intelligent," he told me. "I mean the regulars. The regulars are righteous dudes." To illustrate their perception of differences among prisoners, the regs often mentioned individuals who were not convicts. Kickstand, who spent more than 25 years inside, defined those in the prison population who are not convicts as "inmates, turkeys, lames, lops, rats, punks, child molesters [and] dogs."

In contrast to the regs, the wannabes and drifters frequently characterized convicts as people who were dangerous, fearful, crazy, and different than themselves. Winky, for example, recalled how they frightened him while he was doing time in the 1960s:

> You met these people with these cold understandings—mostly those state raised dudes. They went from Nellis to Tracy [juvenile facilities], then to the adult joint. For them it was all black and white. Those guys scared me 'cause they were stupid. At the same time they were capable of violence.

His statement "they were stupid" indicates he saw himself as outside the mainstream prison culture. A convict, or regular, would view the behavior of the same individuals Winky feared as expected and admirable. Similarly, Brains was shocked at the mere appearance of many California convicts to whom he was exposed in the 1980s: "You had guys with tattoos all over their stomachs, backs and necks. God." Tattoos are common in the CDC and symbolize prisonization. But for him, the tattoos and the meanings found within the convict social world were frightening and ludicrous. He clearly saw himself as an outsider.

RACE, GANGS AND VIOLENCE

Racial hostility and violence are fundamental attributes of prison life in the CDC, which is where most of the fellas did their time. Prison gangs[1] and hometown-related rivalries thrive in California. The unwritten rules of conduct generally prohibit crossing racial lines to establish friendships. Exceptions, though uncommon, are made for individuals who have status and are seen as convicts.

During the interviews, the men often expressed their views regarding the history of gangs in the CDC. A bit of that will be covered here. The rest of the section will be about some of their experiences as they related to racial hostilities on the inside.

California prison gangs (also known as "tips" or "cliques") are based on race, geographical home base, and acceptance of the convict code. These characteristics can come into conflict. Individuals of the same race can be enemies because they come from different geographical locations. Chicanos from the northern part of California have been deadly enemies with Chicanos from the southern region for many years.

Jumbo, a Chicano regular who first did time in the California prison at Soledad in the early 1960s, told me that there was much less of a gang presence back then compared with more recent times. "The cliques were just barely beginning," he told me. "The main Chicano gang back then was from El Paso, Texas," he continued. "Those were the guys who had the drugs." There was also a gang commonly known as the Mexican Mafia (or Eme), which was made up of Chicanos from East Los Angeles. They represented the southern part of the state. The Nuestra Familia (or Ene), which came to be a powerful Chicano gang from northern California in later years, had not yet been formed.

In those earlier days, Chicanos and blacks probably had an easier time fulfilling the cultural mandate. The premier white gang, the Aryan Brotherhood, did not come into being until after the 1960s. Without a structured organization to back them up, whites had to fend for themselves. "White dudes were in trouble [in the 1960s] when they got to Soledad unless they righteously represented themselves or had a small clique to back themselves up," Jumbo recalled.

Gangs like the Black Guerilla Family, and other black groups such as the Black Panthers and Black Muslims emerged in the 1960s as the civil rights movement spilled into the prisons. Winky, a white drifter, remembered the growing Muslim faction. In some ways, he appreciated their presence because it reduced racial tension. "If you were respectful, so were they. So in some ways I was kinda glad to see it happening." However, he felt that because of the strain in race relations, the development of a sense of purpose among blacks was somewhat frightening. "They were scary 'cause they were getting

---

[1] For a brief overview and history of prison gangs, see Leet et al., 1997, 193–230.

organized. In those days there was still a lotta that white devil shit going on." Their efforts and actions were bringing about change within the prison world. This, in turn, created a sense of fear, especially for non-blacks, which was related to the uncertainty their presence would have on the everyday routine of prison life.

Several of the men said they felt the racial differences and animosities that dominate life in California prisons serve the interests of the guards. Their general idea was that as long as prisoners were hating and fighting each other they would not concentrate on the conditions of their lives and their keepers. Baggy, for instance, said, "They want this shit to continue to take the focus off them."

Most of the fellas were never members of prison gangs. Several, in fact, mentioned that they felt conflicts between gangs were senseless. Baggy told me that seeing what was going on during the 1970s between the Nuestra Familia and the Mexican Mafia, who were archenemies by then, was troubling. "It used to trip me out when I was in the joint and I'd see the Nuestra Familia and the Eme. I'd be real conscious about it—wondering what the fuck?" It was hard for him to see people from his hometown become involved. Understanding how Chicanos could hate each other was difficult for him. He explained, "I know it's a macho thing. A lotta pride and stuff. I didn't really express this, 'cause you can't. You're not allowed to. But the view I always held inside me was it was like stupidity."

Only two of the Chicanos I interviewed claimed to have been involved in gangs. Their involvement was perceived as a necessity. For them, membership was a way of attaining status and a means of protection from violence, which often broke out as Chicanos from the northern parts of the state (called "nortenos") battled with Chicanos from the south ("surenos"). Shasta, who had lived in both northern and southern California, told me that by 1979 a Chicano "had to claim one side or the other and if you didn't, you know— fuck, you was on your own." As well as protection, gang membership provided prestige and a positive self-evaluation.

None of the fellas who went to prison in California were able to do their time without being affected by racially based violence. Most had been involved in race riots involving, at a minimum, dozens of prisoners. At the very least, they heard about such things or watched them as they took place. As a result of racial violence, they all had to do "lock down" time, periods in which all prisoners are forced to remain in their cells or dorms, away from the exercise yard and chow hall. They felt these disturbances and their consequences were unavoidable.

Vardo told me about walking into a "tense," racially hostile situation as soon as he got to prison. The first time he went to the exercise yard, he was approached by some other white guys he knew who said there was going to be a riot against the blacks in ten minutes. They told him, "Man, you just start fucking hitting any black dude you see." Sure enough, next thing he knew there was a full-blown riot in progress, guns were going off, tear gas was being thrown onto the yard, and everybody was lying on the ground. "I'm laying face down in scorching hot weather in the dirt," he recalled. Then the goon squad[2] appeared and began physically moving the sprawled out bodies by taking everyone on what he called "a wheelbarrow ride":

> They come around and handcuff you with these plastic handcuffs, and then line everyone up face down. Your face is all dirty, you're all scraped up and the cops are pissed. So they're just picking you up with fucking arms all bent outta' socket, and draggin' you like they're in a wheelbarrow race—two cops on each body.

Their immediate destination was the middle of the yard. "And we were there for hours—knees ripped open, bleeding," he remembered. Approximately 60 men were identified as antagonists. They were taken to administrative segregation—also known as "the hole." The hole is a place where prisoners are segregated from the main population. In theory, one cannot be housed there without violating the rules of the prison. Guilt is determined during a hearing overseen by prison officials.

When confronted by authorities, Vardo pled not guilty to charges of inciting a riot. His plea seemed to anger his accusers. They pressed him for information. One told him, "You tell us what happened. Who told you to do what?" He refused to cooperate. The guards told him that unless he informed them with the information they sought, they were going to let him out of the hole and keep all the other 60 people who were involved in the disturbance locked up. This, they knew, would place him in a double bind. The code required that he remain quiet. So did his integrity. But if the guards released him, it would appear that he had cooperated with them by telling on other prisoners. He remembered a guard telling him, "How's that gonna look to all your homeboys, ratboy? They're gonna know that you told. How do you feel about that?" Being labeled a "rat" in prison can be a death sentence. He remembered thinking, "If these motherfuckers let me out I'll probably get stabbed."

As it happened, he remained quiet and the guards never followed through with their threat. His situation baffled him at first. He thought, "What the fuck is this? This is prison. I'm in prison in prison." He stayed in the hole 37 days. Screams of hate directed at oppositional gangs and racial affiliations were constant during his stay. He recalled some of the sounds, "All night long you hear—'Fuck you nigger.' 'Fuck you, when we get outta here.' 'Southside.' 'Fucking pinche nortenos.'" During his first trip inside a California prison then, Vardo—a drifter—was pulled into a race riot, dragged around the yard by guards, taken to the hole, threatened by guards, and subjected to high levels of verbal animosity between opposing prisoner factions. This all took place within his first 40 days at the institution. It is important to understand that his actions within this context were required by the standards of the prison culture. When he was initially informed that there was going to be a riot, he might have attempted to avoid the conflict. Instead of getting involved, he could have told the guards about the information he had just learned. Either

---

[2] Guards that are called upon to enforce the rules in California prisons are big and aggressive. Convicts call them "goon squads" or "goons" for short.

action, though, would have been grounds for being labeled deviant by other prisoners. By subscribing to the norms of the prison world, he was developing the self-concept of a regular and becoming increasingly more prizonized.

Men from all three groups told me about specific, race-related incidents that, based on their definition of the situation, required them to either threaten or carry out violence against others in prison. Baggy told me about being forced into what he saw as a potentially life-threatening confrontation with another convict. One day, while waiting in line to eat in the chow hall, he was horsing around with two other Chicanos and accidently stepped on the shoes of a black prisoner. His immediate apology was seemingly unheard. The black man was angry and expressed himself outwardly. In response, Baggy's own anger began to build. He remembered his feelings at the time. "He kept on and on and it got me pissed off." He recalled telling the person, "What the fuck you want me to do? Shine your shoes or what?" Behind the black man stood five or six other blacks. The tension in the chow hall, a room containing several hundred men, thickened. "I guess everybody seen what was happening. I remember it getting real quiet," he said. He and his friends left the dining area with the intention of getting ready for battle. He went to his dorm, retrieved a prison-made knife [known as a shank], and returned to the yard in the hot summer sun to resolve the problem. He soon spotted his enemy heading his way. Meanwhile, in preparation of battle, the races began congregating in groups.[3] When his adversary got close enough, he extended his black hand symbolizing his wish to end the conflict without violence. The offer was refused. The black, who was much bigger in size, said, "You know, if I got ahold of you I could kill you right now." Baggy told me he was shaking with fear. Still, he told his foe, "It ain't about fighting. You're dead right now if you want to give it a shot." His statement let the black know he was ready to fight to the death and let a full-scale riot kick off if necessary. Moreover, he was also telling him he had a shank in his possession right then and there. The black gave in claiming to be only two weeks from being paroled. The conflict was over. The public image of the man who backed down was likely weakened. Failure to threaten or carry out violence in specific, often unexpected situations, can lead to stigma and further conflicts from other prisoners. Baggy, on the other hand, having fulfilled the expectations of his world, was able to walk—head high, knowing he did what he had to do to retain his reputation as a convict.

Many stories mentioned during the interviews illustrate the preponderance of violence behind the walls. Brains, for example, said that the amount of racial, gang-related activity he saw while spending 97 days at the CDC's southern California regional reception center at Wasco in 1997 was unbelievable. He had never seen so much violence in such a short time. He mentioned seeing conflicts between blacks known as the Crips and Bloods and extensive hostilities between the Chicano nortenos and surenos. Then there were the Bull Dogs, a newer Chicano group from Fresno. "Originally they were

---

[3] When there is racial tension on the yard that is almost ready to explode into violence, prisoners often congregate, based on their different races, for protection.

nortenos and now they do the dirty work for the surenos," he said. He claimed that he and an old Chicano convict would sit in the yard and watch all the drama going on between these different prisoner factions, which were made up of mostly younger men. They would evaluate specific circumstances and situations and make bets about how long it would take before violence erupted. He said that one time they saw two newly arrived northern Chicanos walking to a dorm. Given that Wasco is a southern prison,[4] the chances they would be confronted by surenos was high. He bet that it would be an hour before they were attacked. His friend guessed it would take less than 30 minutes. Within 20 minutes, the attack was underway and bullets, being shot by guards to break up the melee, were flying. He recalled the experience, "We hit the ground. There were no warning shots then. You had signs posted all over—no warning shots." The goon squad quickly rushed the yard and began taking prisoners. "They were handcuffing guys left and right and they're swinging those batons and yelling," he told me. He remembered once having to "hit the ground" three times in two hours.

The violence found in many prisons today is rampant and likely to continue for quite some time. Some of the fellas' stories support this view. "Doing your own time," "minding your own business" or staying away from trouble while serving a prison sentence, especially in the CDC, may be next to impossible. Wino, a white drifter who had been in the system within the past couple years, concurred. "What it comes down to is this—I don't care how much you try to stay out of it—nowadays, as crazy as it is, you're gonna get involved some way, some how."

REFERENCES TO SELF

In a world devoid of most mainstream activities that affect how people see themselves (for example, wealth, employment, family life), status in prison is based on where one fits within the social hierarchy of the culture. The more one is feared and seen as a regular, the more respect he is given by others, including the guards. In an atmosphere of deprivation and hostility, the ability to maintain respect allows a feeling of superiority and a sense of well being. The following captures how some of the fellas saw themselves as they were pulled deeper into the prison culture.

Becoming a Convict

Compared with the regs, the self-concepts of the drifters and wannabes seemed to be more affected from doing time in prison. The story of Bigwood suggests that, as well as aspiring to be a reg as a youngster, he was almost pushed into seeing himself as a convict as an adult. Much of what he experienced in prison

---

[4] Meaning this is a prison where the surenos have the power. The general policy of the CDC is to separate opposing prisoner factions.

had to do with his large physical size. He mentioned getting involved in weightlifting, a prison activity that has since been stopped because of new CDC policies. "I got into lifting. Always been kinda healthy. And I built up real fast," he remembered. His size gave him the appearance of someone who was capable of violence. He fulfilled the image of a convict without ever taking a violent action. He became seen as a "hog," a term of respect, used to indicate someone who is fearless and strong. Because of the regs he interacted with, his size, and hog status, he was almost revered by guards and other prisoners. He said, "I was like sucked right into it. Now I was hanging out with righteous gangsters. Now I was in the central core of the pen and everyone else is out back. I felt good. I'm in there among men who are stone cold killers and they are showing me respect." He was viewed the same way after being transferred to another prison. He remembered what it was like, "Everyone respected me there. I was the big wood." A "wood" in the CDC is a white, trustworthy, regular.

When considering the way Bigwood was seen and treated in prison, it seems plausible to assume he would eventually internalize the self-concept of a regular. Yet, based on the conversation I had with him, I sensed that he never really came to see himself in such a way. I pursued my hunch by asking him about this. He said I was correct and that he never really saw himself as a fearless, prideful convict. "It was like I'm not really this person. I'm not one of these people. I think I thought I was better than this." The reasons for his confusion may have been related to his early childhood and environmental background, which did not include exposure to the norms of the street. He felt confused because in prison he was somebody with status but on the outside, as a heroin addict, he was a failure. Yet he could not have seen himself as a failure unless he used mainstream values as a point of reference—something a reg would be less likely to do. Claiming that he never really felt like he was "one of these people" suggests he failed to become completely prisonized. This makes sense because though he was seen as a convict, he never took any violent actions against others. He was never truly "tested" to see if he would fulfill the mandates of the convict code. In fact, one of the things he mentioned was that he was always worried about having to "prove himself" by being violent. This fearful thought was always in the back of his mind. "But it just never happened," he recalled. Even though to this day he walks, dresses, and talks like a man who has been in prison for years, in his own mind he does not evaluate himself as a regular.

Several of the drifters and wannabes mentioned that after they completed their first prison sentences they realized they had developed a different view of themselves and the world. This usually involved an adoption of prison values as their own. Vardo said he saw himself differently after his first release. For one thing, he was no longer afraid of doing time. "I knew now that I could make it and what to expect." Moreover, he actually said he enjoyed the experience because it gave him a sense of inclusion within a larger society—something he seemingly never had on the outside. "I started to feel comfortable. I really liked it. Might be strange, but I really felt 'a part of' and accepted there.

I felt I could be trusted. I don't think I was ever a part of anything. I always felt like an outcast my whole life." He talked about how his prison stay helped him become sensitive to racial disturbances. His ability to perceive what was going on helped him deal with the fear that such a hostile environment could potentially create:

> When I saw people grouping I knew the shit [violence] was gonna go down. And after while I didn't even have to see it. It got to be where I could feel it. And shit was always jumping. I knew people were gonna get killed. I knew northern Mexicans and southern Mexicans were gonna club each other to death and the blacks and whites were gonna fight. So for me that was okay 'cause I knew what to expect.

Learning to enjoy doing time might seem absurd. Yet, as Vardo's words suggest, for some people living in prison can actually have benefits. This may be particularly true for individuals who, alienated from the mainstream culture, are able to develop a sense of belonging behind bars.

A few of the drifters indicated that they made conscious efforts to refrain from taking on a convict perspective but failed. They would typically busy themselves with activities apart from the convict culture. Because of a variety of events and unexpected contingencies, though, they found themselves pulled into embracing the meanings of their surroundings. Hippie's story provides a good example. After being arrested for selling LSD to a narcotics officer in the 1960s, he was given an indeterminate sentence of 5 years to life. When he got to prison, he did all he could to retain the meanings and ideas that were related to his hippie self-concept. "I wrote a lot of letters. Tried to keep up the yoga and vegetarianism. Just really tried to maintain the lifestyle I had out there the best I could," he recalled. He said he was living for the outside world, but it was difficult. After he was denied parole for the second year in a row, he realized that he might have to stay in prison for many years. This influenced him to quit resisting the pressures of his environment. As his perspective changed, he started becoming more prisonized. He told me, "I got into what I call convict consciousness. Now I just accepted the fact that I was a convict." His changing self-concept affected his thoughts and actions. He said he started eating meat, lifting weights and looking and talking like all the other convicts. He told me his perceptual shift made his life much easier. "I stopped doing hard time after that. My life was in prison. It was not out there. You do hard time when you're living on the outside in your head."

On The Fringes: Being in the World But Not of It

Not everyone in prison aspires to hang out in the yard, chase drugs, get involved with violence, or otherwise become immersed within the convict culture. In fact, many individuals attempt to protect themselves by carving out private prison world niches or sanctuaries that afford a sense of safety and insulation apart from the main prison activities (Austin and Irwin, 2001,

111–112; Johnson, 1996). These individuals, often short-term prisoners, have generally not been socialized according to the norms of the street (Jones and Schmid, 2000; Johnson, 1996; Schmid and Jones, 1991, 1993). Therefore, they do not see themselves as regulars or convicts.

Several drifters and wannabes talked about doing things that situated them on the fringes of the prison world. Doctor Dee found that becoming familiar with the law and helping other prisoners with legal problems was a way to refrain from hanging out in the yard where most violence takes place. It was also a means of earning respect and compensation. "I learned that you were afforded respect if you knew a little about the law. So I began to make the law my business. I'd do chickenshit things—get demand for trial forms done. Things like that. It was a way of getting respect plus it was a good hustle." Bozo also claimed he did his best to stay away from the everyday, routine activities of the prison. "I always stayed outta' the mix." Like Doctor Dee, he helped other prisoners with legal matters. His efforts provided him with a sense of safety, purpose, and respect. He said, "When I was inside I was a jailhouse lawyer. Nobody fucked with me. Because I had it going on. I had the law books and was trying to get them motherfuckers up outta there. That was my gig." Bozo also taught computer classes and became involved in self-help related activities. "I got into a church thing and a couple drug programs too when I was in there." These men's desire and ability to find niches apart from mainline prison activities helped them resist the pressures of prisonization.

The way the fellas who lived on the fringes of the prison culture evaluated themselves had a lot to do with their ability to withstand the pull of the convict social world. Their interviews indicated they saw themselves as different and usually better than the regulars. Brains, for example, told me he did his best to refrain from convict-related activities. At one point, he did 56 months in a Nevada prison for possession of heroin. His experience there did little to prepare him for the harsh realities of the California Rehabilitation Center (CRC) where he was later sentenced for another drug conviction. While at CRC he worked as an education clerk. His job kept him apart from the mainline population part of the time. Yet, because he was housed in a dorm environment, he was often surrounded by what he perceived to be the deviant activities of other prisoners. He told me that people at CRC were extremely dangerous compared with those who surrounded him while he was locked up in Nevada. "In California it's more serious. These boys are for real. They talk about that tension. You can feel that tension. Gang affiliations—it's just different." He characterized his California prison time as humiliating. Comparing himself with others at CRC, he said, "I thought I was so much better than that." He saw California convicts who were addicts, and the actions they took, as disgusting. He recalled a few reasons why:

> It was their scandalous moves. I mean everything. It made me sick. Guys burning guys for their tobacco. They're hustling up enough canteen [items

such as cigarettes purchased at the prison store] to score.[5] And people were hooked. It's not a rehabilitation center. It's a prison. Guys getting killed. The outfits [syringes] they'd use. The things they'd do to get loaded.

Men like him who did not identify as convicts and lived on the fringes of this deviant social setting seemed to see themselves as being in the world of prison, but not of it.

Release

The prison experience can have a crippling effect on the chances for a successful reintegration to society. Jim Austin and John Irwin sum it up nicely:

> For decades, students of the prison have recognized that the combined factors of being isolated from outside society, subjected to a reduced and deprived routine, and acculturated into a unique "convict" belief and value system work to "prisonize" men and women—that is, convert them into persons equipped to live in prison and ill equipped to live outside. (Austin and Irwin, 2001, 109–110)

Prisoner advocates emphasize a need to alter the structural impediments (for example, loss of civil rights, blocked employment opportunities) that hinder an individual's chances of making a successful transition from prison to the outside world (Richards, 1995). Such arguments are important. Yet, how one evaluates himself after getting out and how he thinks others see him will greatly affect his actions and chances for success. Moreover, the more prisonized he is, the more he will use the prison culture as his reference group when making judgements and decisions on the outside. A prisonized perspective is perhaps the greatest obstacle to overcome before one can make it in the free world after release.

Several of the fellas talked about experiencing "culture shock" after getting out of prison. They typically felt out of place wherever they went. Simple things like walking into a supermarket or speaking to a woman could bring about high levels of self-consciousness and anxiety. Many of their feelings were related to how they felt others were perceiving them. Vardo recalled thinking that, "Everyone looked at me like they were scared to death." Their fear was likely influenced by his appearance. The style of his clothes, walk, and general demeanor, a reflection of the prison culture, were symbolic of a dangerous individual. He said he figured they thought, "Jesus Christ. Charles Manson just got out." The way he believed they saw him left him with mixed emotions. He felt good because he sensed their fear gave him status and power. At the same time, he felt bad because the women he saw reminded him of his sisters. "They reminded me of normal people," he recalled. After Vardo asked Huero

---

[5] To "score" is to obtain drugs. The "scandalous" moves mentioned take place in every prison and street drug culture I have seen. To "burn" somebody is to falsely promise to provide drugs for some amount of money (or other commodity). Like, "Give me the money. Wait right here. I'll be right back with the dope."

if he felt out of place after getting out, Huero said, "Yeah, but in an elitist sort of way." His response is understandable. Those who were prisonized brought convict perspectives to the outside world. Their sense of alienation, though fearful, was not life threatening. The people they generally encountered in the free world, unless they were cops, were not really frightening because they were not perceived as being capable of violence as were their enemies on the inside. In this regard then, though they felt alienated, they evaluated themselves as from a superior position.

Several of the fellas who did not become highly prisonized talked about how difficult it was making the transition from prison to the free world. Wino told me that the effects of getting out were overwhelming. Occasionally, he said, he would make plans to "do good" after he was paroled. "A few times I'd save the dollar a day [his daily wage] I was making to do good when I got out so I'd have money to get a place, get a job, and do everything right." Yet, his plans were hindered, in part, by the high degree of alienation he felt when exposed to people in the free world. From his view, they looked at him like a stranger in a strange land. "Soon as I got out, everyone is looking at me. It was like everyone knew I'd been to prison. It was like being from another planet."

One of the major obstacles newly released prisoners face is the stigma they perceive being directed toward them and its effect on their self-evaluations. Being released can entail a severe sense of alienation. The reason for this is, once released, prisoners continue to define situations from the standpoint they shared with others when they were inside (Shibutani, 1986). As when I saw my old friend Max shortly after he was released, the outside world is perceived through prisonized eyes.

5

Ways Out: Breaking
the Patterns

The Redefinition of Self as
Motivation to Change

With the passing of time, new associations, and the ongoing development of a meaning system reflecting the values of the street and the
penitentiary, my own heroin-using career took on distinctive characteristics.
After becoming addicted, it never took me too long to get re-arrested. Once
in custody, I would go through the detox process, settle into the rounds and
routines of incarceration, and eventually be paroled. Once released, always
with the thought in mind that I never wanted to return to prison, I would
make an effort to stay out of trouble. Often, but not always, this included
trying to stay away from heroin. My success in this regard wavered. During
some periods, I failed miserably. On one occasion, I was arrested within two
weeks for shoplifting. During others, I did fairly well. Ultimately, though, I
always ended up getting hooked again, and not long thereafter, I'd be back in
custody.

My last arrest, as noted earlier, resulted in a six-and-a-half-year trip behind
bars in Oregon. During that time, I was fortunate enough to spend two years
in a college program where the foundation of my worldview began to crum-
ble. I started to see myself as something much more than merely an out of
control addict/criminal. As never before, I began getting glimpses of my life as
it existed within a broad sociohistorical context. As never before, I began en-
tertaining possibilities about my future that extended beyond the street or the
yard, possibilities impossible to imagine in days gone past.

When I was within a year of release, the prison officials at the "release center"[1] I was housed in began awarding me "passes" to the outside world. Designed, I assume, to ease the transition to the free world, these passes were like a legal get-out-of-prison-free card. All I had to do was sign a piece of paper saying I would not break any laws and promise to return in two days, and I was allowed to leave from Friday to Sunday night.

By the time I went on my first pass, I had been locked up more than five years. By then, the only people I knew on the outside in that state were people I had gotten to know in prison before their own releases. So into their lives I went. Most of my pass time was spent with Shakes, a guy I lived in the same cell with (a cellie) for many months while he was locked up. He had his own home, a live-in girlfriend, a van, and a job as a carpet layer. Instead of heroin, though, Shakes was a speed freak. Methamphetamine was his drug of choice. Before he picked me up for my first pass, I told him I could not use any narcotics out there because they would likely give me a drug test when I returned. A dirty test would mean an instant trip back to maximum security, which is where I would stay until I paroled.

The few passes I made to Shakes' house were a disaster. It was bad enough experiencing the culture shock of being "out." But he and others I came into contact with during those times made it even harder. Speed freaks do strange things like stay awake for days and even weeks, eat little food, and spend hours in the mirror picking their faces. Shakes was one of those guys that made these weird noises that seemed to come from his throat or nasal passages while he was on one of his sleepless journeys. While laying carpet, which I helped him do several times, he might spend three or four hours ironing down one seam to make it perfect. His girlfriend, who was extremely thin, would do things like continuously clean the house or spend hours fidgeting with items in what appeared to be a jewelry box. One evening at around 9 P.M. I cooked up some eggs, bacon, and toast, and tried to share some with her. She politely refused, telling me she had already eaten that day. When I asked her if she was talking about the half cup of dry Lucky Charms I saw her eating earlier that morning, she said yes. The point here is that compared to the way I saw the world, these people were gone. From my perspective, speed freaks made even hard-core heroin addicts from the street seem like model citizens.

The more passes I took, the more out of place I felt in the outside world. As on previous occasions when I had been released, the more alienated I felt the less I cared about trying to "do good." One Friday I made it to Shakes' house to find him and his girlfriend to be deeply depressed. Their dark dispositions stemmed from the fact that they were broke and out of speed. On Sunday, the day I was to return to the release center, I suggested we go shoplifting. As luck would have it, I got caught. Now here I was, arrested while on a pass from prison. While in the holding tank of the Portland jail, I met an old California

---

[1] The release center was a minimum-security institution with decent living conditions. The major means of control used by staff there was the threat of being sent back to "the walls," the old maximum security prison where I spent most of my time, for rule violations.

convict who just happened to have a pocketful of speed. After snorting a few lines, which he generously offered to share with me, I felt like I was on Pluto. Since I had told the police my real name and the fact that I was on a pass from the release center, I figured it was only a matter of time until I would be taken back to the walls. Instead, to my great surprise, they released me to the streets.

Back then, people who failed to return from a pass were placed on escape status. When caught, however, they were not charged with a new offense. The only thing that really happened was we were not given credit for doing prison time while on escape. The clock merely stopped while we were gone. Knowing this, and knowing I would be sent back to maximum security if I did return to the release center, I decided to stay out awhile.

The result of all this was about a 90-day vacation in speed-freak hell. The longer I stayed out, the worse it got. Toward the end, Shakes and a friend were trying to make some speed themselves in his kitchen. The problem was they had no idea what they were doing. Without having any actual recipe for "cooking" the drug, they based their actions on speculation and trial and error. Into a large pot went some basic ingredients such as chicken food designed to increase egg productivity, red devil lye, and muriatic acid. As I sat watching, listening to Shakes uttering these weird noises, I saw green fumes rising from the pot. The friend suggested they tear up some aluminum foil into small pieces and place them in the pot. "If the foil disappears," he said with excitement, "we'll have us a reaction!" The next thing I know, these guys are hurriedly tearing Reynolds Wrap into tiny pieces. The aluminum foil scenario was the kicker. I felt incredulous, like I belonged with these people in this place about as much as an African American belongs in a Ku Klux Klan rally. All I could think was, "What the hell am I doing here?"

The next day the three of us ventured out to lay some carpet. On the way to the job, Shakes pulled his van into the parking lot of a shopping mall. "Why are we here," I asked. They told me they were going to a store that sold pool supplies because they needed an instrument to measure the "ph" levels (whatever that meant) of the speed they were still planning on making. Feeling frustrated, and utterly disillusioned, I entered the mall with them through a Target store. It was my intention to steal something so it could later be returned for cash while they went and looked for their instrument. My effort was unsuccessful. Before long I was apprehended and standing in a security room of the mall. In the midst of all the video monitors aimed at potential suspects, the security guard informed me that I became a suspect as soon as I entered the store. He told me it was not me so much, but the two characters I walked in with. What immediately came to mind was what Shakes and his friend must have looked like on one of the video monitors. Both of them had hair that was extended outward in every imaginable direction and a look that reflected their spaced out mental condition. When the regular police came, they already knew I was on escape status. Rather than being transported to jail for petty theft, I was taken directly back to the main state prison and never charged. Once I got to a cell on the fifth tier of E-block and lay down on the bunk, I felt a tremendous sense of relief. Instead of being in what seemed like hell, I felt like I was home. As I comfortably laid down on the thin, green, institutional mattress atop the slab of steel that was my bed, I somehow realized deep down in my gut that I never had to live out there in a state of total senselessness, desperation, and futility again.

My excursion to the outside world at that time became a significant event in my life. It helped me recognize how much different I had become since attending college and spending all those years in custody. It helped me see, in short, that my aspirations had changed because I was no longer the person I used to be.

THE FELLAS AND THE PROCESS
OF CHANGE

The development of new perspectives, about oneself and the world, are most often necessary precursors to dramatic behavioral change. This process includes a reinterpretation of meanings related to one's self-assumptions. The likelihood that new lines of action will be sought increases when these assumptions, many which have never been questioned, are either shattered or seen in a different light. A prisonized individual in the prime of his life might, for example, see himself as a respected figure within the prison culture because he has many convict friends and is seen as trustworthy. Yet, such a view would be difficult to retain if the respect he received was lost because, say, he violated the convict code or could not act violently because he developed a physically debilitating condition. In other words, when the positive attributes used to define oneself lose their meaning, it becomes almost necessary to establish a new self-concept and worldview (Charmaz, 1991; personal conversations with Tamotsu Shibutani, 1999).

Perhaps the most generally accepted explanation for the desistance of deviant behavior is the "maturing out" hypothesis, which claims that as people grow older they do less crime (Gottfredson and Hirschi, 1990; Herrnstein and Wilson, 1985). Similarly, evidence suggests that as people age they leave behind lifestyles centered around heroin addiction (Snow, 1973; Winick, 1962). Generally, the older they get, the more their ideas reflect mainstream values. Basically, they "grow up." This process is often explained as being related to marriages or jobs that have meaning in people's lives (Sampson and Laub, 1993). Yet, it is the way people see themselves within these relationships that pushes the change.

Studies of the de-addiction process commonly find that "bottoming-out" is a crucial precursor to behavioral change for addicts (Brill, 1972; Coleman, 1975; Ebaugh, 1988; Snow, 1973; Stall and Biernacki, 1986; Waldorf, 1970). Bottoming-out generally includes experiencing some degree of suffering that serves as a motivation to seek another way to live. Although this will be a personal, subjective experience, reasons for bottoming-out include economic desperation, personal isolation, experiences in the criminal justice system, bad health, and guilt (Coleman, 1975).

Hitting bottom is often associated with a significant event that becomes a turning point in a person's life. A significant event stands out in one's memory because it has boundaries, intensity, and great personal meaning. It should be noted that the meaning of the event evolves after it happens and becomes solidified as it is retold over time. Sorting out the meaning of such events, as I did by telling the story about my vacation in hell, helps explain why they are seen as turning points (Charmaz, 1991).

Many of these generally accepted components regarding the process of change were common among the lives of the fellas. Generally, they all got older, tired, and eventually hit some form of bottom. By the time they made the decision to find a better way to live, their self-concepts were much different than when, for example, they first started using drugs and going to prison.

Patterns

Though their experiences varied, the fellas spent years developing behavioral patterns that revolved around doing time and using heroin. For the most prisonized, the general pattern seemed to be spending the majority of their time behind bars where drugs would be used as much as possible.[2] Their prison time would be interrupted by brief trips to the outside world where drug use would be pursued. Shortly thereafter, they would get arrested, and once again find themselves in jail going through the court process. Once they were returned to prison, the cycle would be complete. Pelon summarized his pattern: "For me, pretty much everything stayed the same. I'd go to the pen, get out, and use drugs. I never stopped using drugs. The only difference was it was always less when you're in jail."

Several of the men told me their patterns were affected by their contempt for rules, regulations, or legal representatives of the state. These antagonistic views are understandable considering the degradation ceremonies they experienced as convicts and parolees. Doctor Dee, who became fairly prisonized, claimed that his pattern left little room for respect of the law. He said he would go to jail, get out, and use heroin as much as possible until he was re-arrested and returned to custody. When I asked him if he ever made any effort to "do good" after being released, he almost laughed. With a sense of disdain that remains to this day, he answered, "No. I never even reported to the parole officer. I'd fix in the parking lot right after getting out if I could."

The fellas' patterns often involved relationships with women. A few were married at one time or another. Two, Junior and Hippie, managed to maintain long-term marriages despite their heroin-using careers. Most of them, however, had fleeting relationships, many which would dissolve after they got arrested. Kickstand, who did roughly 25 years behind bars, talked about his pattern as it related to women. He expected any female companion left behind after he got arrested to get together with another male heroin addict

---

[2] Contrary to popular belief, there are not more drugs in prison than on the outside. Much of this is because the supply can never meet the demand.

until he was paroled. That way she could get help taking care of her drug habit. Such relationship dynamics were seen as unfortunate but inevitable. But as soon as he would get out, if he were lucky, "she would come back to daddy." Once back together, she would work as a prostitute while he committed petty thefts to keep them going. This would continue until the relationship broke up or another arrest would take place. Though relationships with women came and went, the pattern never changed. In its completed state, he would once again find himself in prison.

Like other heroin addicts, many of the fellas' behavioral patterns included working at legitimate jobs (Faupel and Klockars, 1987). Their mostly blue-collar occupations included maintenance, construction, welding, and factory work. Bozo, however, worked as a computer analyst. After getting released from custody, he would find employment as a consultant. "They didn't care about my record. They were interested in what I could do," he recalled. Once he got paid, he would buy some heroin and then go "party" at a nightclub where he would try to meet women. As his habit increased, his activities changed. Before long, partying was no longer part of the picture. By then, he said, all his time would be spent "trying to get that dollar to get that next motherfuckin' fix." Along with work, Bozo's pattern included forging checks. He told me, "That was the cycle up 'til the next bust [arrest]. Then you got busted again, got a new bit [more prison time from the judge] and went back upstate [back to prison]." Doctor Dee claimed that his pattern included work and a multitude of parole violations. While in prison he would get healthy. As soon as he got out, he would go back to work and begin using heroin again. "I'd go back to work for this company as a pipe fitter. They always had a spot for me. And I got paid good there," he remembered. Regardless of their efforts to earn money by working, these men inevitably returned to prison for drug-related crimes.

Redefinition of the Self as a Motivation to Change

Heavy drug users seldom decide to voluntarily alter their lifestyles unless they begin to see themselves and their actions in a negative light. "Any addict will affirm that only those who fail in the drug world will consider a change in lifestyle" (Coombs, 1981, 383). Before making the decision to quit using heroin and seek a new direction in life, the fellas generally developed a dismal view of themselves as human beings. Several became chronically incarcerated, chronically unemployable, or extremely sick. In short, the general course of their lives took a downward spiral over time.

Sick, Tired, and Almost Dead. Many of the fellas said that before they got clean, they got so sick they could barely function. Several almost died. The assumptions Kickstand had about himself, for example, took on new meaning with the onset of health problems and old age. After asking what motivated him to quit using drugs and alcohol, he said, "I'm just tired, man. My health's shot. Had a couple heart attacks. About killed myself." Wino told me that just before getting clean, he was addicted to both heroin and alcohol, homeless, seldom ate, was extremely unhealthy and living underneath a freeway. He said one day, shortly after awakening, he felt strange after helping a friend finish the better part of a fifth of vodka. "I felt weird that morning. I felt different. My equilibrium was off. I could think okay, but I couldn't walk or talk." He thought he just needed some heroin to make everything return to normal. After injecting some into his body, however, he overdosed. He remembered, "It took a long time to come out of it in the hospital." Shortly thereafter, he found himself in jail again. There, he finally realized he had to quit using drugs and alcohol or else he would die. "That's what it had to come down to for me. It wasn't like I could walk into an AA meeting at the age of 22 and get sober. I had to go through all that other shit and get to the point where I knew if I kept using and drinking I'd die."

The fellas often mentioned that they noticed they were getting older before they got clean. Sometimes this occurred while they were living outside of prison. They began realizing, for example, that others who were using heroin and other drugs were younger than themselves. Most often, though, they became aware of their age while they were locked up. Kickstand told me that the last time he was in jail, he thought they put the wrong wristband on him (prisoner photographs are placed on their wrists for purposes of identification). Looking at his own photograph left him stunned. He remembered the moment, "Fuck, I looked at that dude [himself] and thought, 'Jesus man, they fucked up and got some other guy's picture on there. That ain't me.'" He did not recognize himself because he looked older than he imagined himself to be. Bozo recalled being referred to as "Pop," a term indicating one is old, by younger prisoners in New York. He remembered not appreciating their use of the word:

> I remember the last bit I did. Those motherfuckers called me Pop. Called me fucking Pop, man. I knew my motherfucking ass was old. You know what I'm saying? Fuckin' Pops. I said, "Shit, I ain't your motherfucking father dude. Call me no fucking Pops. Popsickle. Pop this bitch."

The downward spirals of the fellas were affected by unexpected contingencies. Their narratives frequently revealed times when they endured great degrees of pain, fear, and inner turmoil from situations and events they did not anticipate and could not control. The experiences that followed often propelled them toward unprecedented depths of desperation and despair. The following story is a good example.

After years of working, hiding his drug use from family members, and going in and out of jail and prison for drug related activities, Bigwood experienced an unexpected event which was still painful at the time of the interview. His mother died. Her death was devastating. From his view, she was the only person in his life who loved him unconditionally. Shortly after she died, he lost his job working for the city. He cashed out and spent all his public employees savings on heroin. Next, he began doing crimes to support his habit. "I went on the rampage, writing bad checks, hanging paper [forgeries]," he told me. His level of desperation escalated. He recalled the period:

> I'm out stealing, hustling—doing everything to maintain a habit after my mom died. I mean, just barely getting away with stealing. My pants are falling off [because he was so skinny and malnourished]. My face is sucked up [thin]. I'm not shaving. I mean, I'm the scum of the dopefiends.

At this painful point in his life, he evaluated himself as deficient, inadequate, afraid, and desperate. He even saw himself as morally inferior to other addicts. Then he caught what has been called "the flesh eating disease"—an ailment that affects addicts who inject tainted heroin into their muscles rather than their veins. The fear he subsequently experienced was not without merit. He recalled knowing about the potential effects of the disease from friends who had been infected. "Another dude who I was just fixing with a few weeks before—his foot was almost eaten off by this flesh eating thing. Someone else I knew had just died four days before from this same stuff." Soon he found himself in the hospital where, according to the doctors, he might easily have died. One night, because of being in extreme agony, he ripped out all the tubes they had placed into his body. He remembered the pain:

> I was crying, screaming, punching the walls. I was in agony. They did surgery. One doctor told me that they'd had a few people die from this infection. They called my family and told them if I made it through the night I might have a chance. I mean, it was bad. I just wanted to die—to give up.

Next, he had what has been called a "mysticoreligious" or "near death" experience—a moment in which a new awareness about the self helps one realize the detrimental costs of his or her actions (Stall and Biernacki, 1986). He told me that while he was asleep he almost died:

> I felt all these little demon feet and pressure on my chest. This is the God's honest truth. Whether anybody believes me or not. I felt my breathing getting sucked down. I was just sitting there, my eyes wide open, but the shutters started going down. I felt this pressure on my chest. I couldn't breathe. I was on my way out. And at the last second I popped up like something just pulled me up right out of there.

Still in bad shape by the time he left the hospital, he attempted to recuperate at his father's house but was told he would not be welcome there until he quit getting high. Homeless and in miserable condition, he continued using the drug he believed was the cause of all his problems. Perhaps it was the only relief he could find in his fear-encompassed world:

> I was just fucked up. I hated life. I hated everybody. I thought, "What am I gonna do." Crying to myself. "That fucking heroin. I hate this shit. I'll never be nothing. I'll just be a bum." I didn't know what to do. Too scared to live on the streets. Too scared to do anything. I mean I was really fearful about everything.

Not long thereafter, he sought treatment in a live-in drug program.

Cheap Wine, Dereliction, and No Place Else to Go. Several of the fellas told me that toward the later stages of their drug-using careers, they replaced heroin with alcohol because it is legal, cheaper, and requires less effort to obtain. Like heroin, the "pull" or addictive nature of alcohol can be very strong. It can also be characterized by deep levels of despair. Doctor Dee claimed that toward the end of his downward spiral, he seldom used heroin. Instead, he drank cheap, white port wine. He attempted to keep his life together by working when he could, and by maintaining relationships with women. Yet, there were times he felt he could no longer stand the pressures of life. When the turmoil became too much to handle, he sought sanctuary in an unexpected place. "One day I just walked away from it all and went straight to the bushes," he told me. It was a place he felt safe. He could drink his wine and nobody, not even his girlfriend, could bother him there. As time passed, his trips to the bushes became more common. His health was also deteriorating. Eventually, no longer able to work, he began panhandling (begging) for a living and the bushes became his permanent home. He explained what it was like, "So I'm in the bushes—can tell I'm getting pancreatitis. I'd run outta money. My hustle became panhandling." His downward spiral was not yet complete. Before long, no longer able to even beg, he manipulated himself into a situation where he could live off the panhandling proceeds of a mentally ill individual who he met in the bushes:

> So what I did was—I had some urine soaked mattress off in the bushes and I subleased half of it to a card carrying nut. I mean just a certified nut. And I'd get him up at 5:30 A.M. to go what I called fishing. I'd send him out trolling, panhandling, and I'd take the money. I'd buy the wine, and I'd let him hang out with me. That was the trade off.

At this point in time, his self-concept reflected the hopeless, degrading conditions of his life:

> So I don't know what to do. I wanna die, but I'm afraid to die. I just know I can't live like this anymore. I keep thinking about that army commercial, "Be all that you can be." And I think, "Man, you're just a piece of shit." My self-esteem is nonexistent.

Shortly thereafter, he made an effort to seek an alternative way of living.

The story of Winky is similar. For years, he worked in a Del Monte plant making catsup. As a member of the Teamster's union, he earned decent wages and was able to generally refrain from serious criminal activity. As he grew older, he began replacing heroin with alcohol. "Drinking became more and more what I did as time went by," he said. He realized that the wine was as addicting as heroin. "For me, the minute I drank any I'd have to get more if I had any choice about it. Steal it—whatever. That wine had me hooked like a dog just like junk [heroin] did." His alcohol habit was taking him steadily downward. By the time the plant he worked in closed, his pattern of drinking left him unable to find new employment. Eventually he found himself living only for wine, doing whatever he could to get it, and homeless. He remembered segments of his bottom. "By the end I was a sweet wine alcoholic. I was living on the street. Scuffling. Begging for change. Petty thieving." Living on the streets, eating out of dumpsters, begging for quarters, and drinking cheap wine became his normal routine. He told me sometimes he would sleep "wherever I fell down." Toward the end he was running around with a guy named Bob who looked over at him one day and said, "You know, we're dying. You know that?" And Winky said, "Yeah, I can feel it." Bob told him that when he got his social security check on the first of the month they should leave Sacramento and go to Santa Barbara to get sober. He agreed. But, he told me, his real interest was Bob's money. "I said, 'Okay.' Had no idea what he was talking about really. He coulda' said, 'Lets go to Denver and get drunk' and I woulda said yeah. Was kinda focused in on him getting that money." Once Bob got paid, they traveled to Santa Barbara. After a few days of being very drunk, Bob got up from the ground they were laying on and said he had to go somewhere—that he would find him later. Winky, too drunk to follow, said okay. The next day he came up with the idea to call AA on the telephone to see if he could find Bob. He was told that they had a lot of Bobs in AA. Over the phone, he met a woman who encouraged him to come and see her. She took him to an AA meeting, and he has been sober ever since. He never saw Bob again. That was 16 years ago. His trip to Santa Barbara was the result of an unexpected contingency, something that could never have been planned or predicted. If it had not been for Bob, he might never have gotten sober. The trip to Santa Barbara and the phone call to the woman at AA were turning points in his life.

Redefining the Self Within the Prison Culture: Losing the Convict Mystique. During the interviews, several of the fellas talked about how they came to see themselves differently while they were locked up. Most of these were regs or individuals who became highly prisonized. Wheels said that at the age of 47, he contracted a rare illness that greatly diminished his physical capabilities. "I had to learn to walk all over again. I didn't have any feelings in my hand. I used walkers, crutches, wheelchairs." Though he saw himself as a convict and had status within the prison, his weakened physical condition affected his thinking. He became increasingly fearful about his safety. "I started getting paranoid because I couldn't back myself up [fight] in a violent society. I became more and more paranoid," he recalled. He also began worrying about being retaliated against for actions he had taken against others in the past. "I started thinking of people that I'd hurt—that now they were gonna get me. I was thinking of people I had robbed on the streets and thought they were gonna get word to people inside. They were gonna throw things in my cell, burn me up." His level of fear became so intense that he eventually asked the guards to place him in protective custody. "Locking up" in such a fashion is looked at with contempt by convicts. Protective custody inmates (known as PC cases) are housed in isolated prison locations and are highly stigmatized within the prison culture. Many are sex offenders and informants.

Wheels' first stop was the Psychiatric Security Unit (PSU) where, though physically safe, he felt humiliation and shame. His request to be housed in protective custody meant he could never again be seen and treated as a convict. He defined the meaning of his action:

> Now, you have to realize, this is me the convict, tough guy his whole life. My whole persona rested on being a convict. And I locked up. To lock up in prison goes against the code. We're talking tribal stuff here. I broke the code. I was banished from my tribe.

The fear he was experiencing because of his physical condition, coupled with the fact that he had placed himself in protective custody, contradicted the premises upon which his convict self-concept was built. Convicts are not scared. Convicts do not "lock up."

From PSU, he was sent to the state hospital and placed in a program for the mentally and emotionally disabled. After two years of participation in treatment-oriented activities (such as counseling and group therapy) at this program, he got into minor trouble and was sent back to the main prison population for a short period. While in the yard, he was confronted by others and called a rat because he had gone to the treatment program. Prisoners in treatment programs are often stigmatized by convicts. Taking part in any type of program that encourages behavioral change is seen as a symbol of weakness and evidence of a willingness to adhere to the wishes of authorities. He remembered being ostracized. "They were calling me names that weren't true. Now I was a rat. I mean, I hadn't ratted on nobody. But if you're in treatment you're a rat." He felt conflicted. On the one hand, he still saw himself as a convict but now he was also "wanting to be a citizen" (normal). He said most of the people in the prison still treated him with respect, but "the higher echelon" considered him an outcast. Being seen as a pariah by the same group of people he had identified with most of his life had the effect of putting the nail in the coffin of his convict identity. "I did twelve long, hard, miserable days in there that time. And it took all the glamour the prison had—took it out, it was gone."

Wheels could no longer be a convict. The illness he contracted was an unexpected contingency, a turning point, and a significant event that greatly affected the course of his life. Today, he sees it as being the central reason for his change. "Now I look at my illness as a great gift. If it hadn't of happened and I kept this 6-foot-2-inch, 190-pound body that could maintain the persona of a convict, I probably would have. I was pretty successful at it. It was all I knew."

Another representation of how some of the fellas came to redefine themselves within the prison culture came from Rabbit who, in his middle thirties, found himself beginning a 10-year sentence for armed robbery. Though he saw himself as a convict, he no longer enjoyed doing time as he did when he was younger. The thought of completing 10 calenders behind the walls seemed deplorable. Having been in jail for roughly 9 months before arriving in prison, he was already tired of being locked up, and his sentence had just begun. To divert his attention from the feelings of misery and helplessness he was experiencing, he started talking to another convict about trying to escape from the institution. As this was going on, he began having a series of dreams. His father, who passed away when he was 13 years old, would appear in the dreams and attempt to steer him in a different direction. His interpretation of the dreams, especially the last one, had a great impact on his thinking:

> Over the course of about a year I had these dreams that really stuck in my mind—where my dad was tryin' to tell me something. And the last dream woke me up—I mean in a cold sweat. I remember being in this cave in this dream. And there were three witches—stirring this pot. And they were talking about me as if I weren't there. I guess they were gonna boil me in the fucking pot or something, you know. And they were laughing. And I'm a boy of about 13—the age I was when my dad died—and all of a sudden my dad appears and he's got me by the shoulders and he's going, "Boy, you're not getting it. You're not gonna make it. You're not understanding what I'm trying to tell you and you're not gonna make it." That fucking dream woke me up, man, and I was sweating like a motherfucker. That dream changed me. I paid attention to that dream.

Rabbit's dream can be seen as another example of a "mysticoreligious" experience (Stall and Biernacki, 1986)—an unexpected contingency interpreted today as a significant event. Importantly, he associated the meaning of the dreams with his yearning for a different perspective. He said, "I look at that dream, or that series of dreams, as where I changed. Something in me changed from that point on. And I really got into the spiritual stuff then. I was searching for some answers." In search of new meanings, he withdrew from the escape plans, began reading books about spirituality, and attending college classes in the education department—activities that might facilitate a new view of oneself and the world.

With the passing of time, Rabbit's perception did change. He started to see convicts differently and began to critically examine their value system:

> I lost that whole convict mystique and started re-evaluating that whole thing, man, during that time there. I started looking around me and listening to the conversations that were going on at the chow table and out on the yard [major places of prisoner socialization]. And I'm realizing that this is a fucking, upside down, skewed view of life going on here. I mean, these ideas that are floating around in here—bouncing off walls. They sound real good. But they don't have any substance.

He got to the point where he no longer saw himself as a convict. He recalled his thoughts, "I'm lookin' at these guys thinking, 'I'm not like that guy. And, what's more, I don't wanna be like that guy.'" For Rabbit, being in prison had become so painful that he began seeking some way out of his deplorable situation. From that pain came an eventual reinterpretation of the values and norms common to the prison culture and the motivation to find new meanings about himself and the world.

Redefining the Self Within the Prison Culture: Where Did All the Convicts Go? A handful of the regs talked about how they began to notice that the prison culture itself was changing and that convicts, as they knew them, were disappearing. Consequently, the forces that had acted to bolster their own self-concepts were becoming extinct.

From the time they were young, these regs had been accustomed to being locked up with guys they knew from their neighborhoods. One of the things they mentioned was that many of these people were no longer around. As Pelon told me, "Most of 'em died. Very few stopped using drugs or anything like that. Most died in overdoses or robberies or getting killed inside." As time passed and their social circles dwindled, these men found themselves more and more isolated within the prison world.

The regs also talked about how the quality of their lifestyles behind bars had deteriorated over time because of the different types of people being sent to prison. They typically said that "in the old days," which usually meant the 1960s and 1970s, it seemed that almost everyone who got locked up was a heroin addict. Individuals got along better then, they claimed, and there was much less gang activity. Along with increased gang activity, which had a great affect on their everyday lives, they talked about an onslaught of new types of guards. Jumbo told me that during the 1990s they seemed to have gotten younger. "It was like they were right outta' high school." They also mentioned that the level of prisoner/guard interaction had increased and become more friendly. In the old days, convicts generally talked to guards only when they needed something, such as permission to sign up for a phone call. More recently, they noticed prisoners of all types engaging the guards in friendly conversation.

It was also mentioned that in recent years California prisons were being overrun by people who, before, would have never been sent there. Kickstand said, "A lotta guys today don't belong there. Now you're getting a lot of drunk drivers and mental cases." They claimed that rapists, and other types of sex offenders, were now being housed in the main prison population. Before, they were placed in protective custody. Not only that, these new inmate types, I was told, competed with each other to see who would inform on one another first. To make matters worse, from the perspective of the regs, these actions were seldom reprimanded by convicts. Huero explained the problem by saying that in the old days, "rats were either stabbed or not allowed on the yard. Nobody does nothing anymore. It's fucked up." Pelon told me about an older guard who approached him and suggested he no longer belonged in prison. He recalled the guard's words, "You're one of the very last convicts, man. Not too many of you guys left. People don't know how to act around here anymore. I'm retiring pretty quick. You should think about doing the same."

As a result of the changes in the wider society, especially the "get tough" on crime and drugs political climate beginning in the early 1980s, and the subsequent changes in their prison worlds, these men found themselves in an unfamiliar environment. Rather than being able to enjoy the benefits reserved for those at the top of the prison social hierarchy, as they had in days gone by, they were becoming outsiders in the eyes of others and themselves.

A Prison Epiphany. Of all the fellas interviewed, only Vardo characterized the change in his life as being related to an epiphany that he explained as being a sudden flash of recognition about himself that he now interprets as a turning point in his life.

As a youngster, Vardo came from a middle-class family. Though he dabbled in drug use as an adolescent, he was never incarcerated as a juvenile. Spending time behind bars did not become part of his lifestyle until he began using heroin as an adult. By the time he was in his early thirties, he knew how to walk the walk, talk the talk, and play the games of convicts. After several trips to jail and prison, he came to see himself as a reg.

One day, after shooting some heroin in a dorm, he stepped out onto the second tier of the prison he was in and looked out over the yard. From where he stood, he noticed the guard towers, a group of black prisoners singing together, some Mexicans playing soccer, and people exercising on the weight pile. He also saw two Chicanos talking to each other. One appeared to be about 18 and the other around 60 years old. The clothes of both men were pressed, their shirts were buttoned to the top, and they carried themselves like regs. The thoughts that followed his definition of the situation became, to him, a major turning point. Then and there, he claims to have realized that unless he personally did something to alter the course of his life, he would find himself in prison doing the same thing at 60 as he was doing that day. He thought, "Fuck. This is my life. It ain't never gonna change. It's just gonna be the same." He believed his use of heroin was at the root of all his problems. He remembered thinking, "And I can't even stop using [heroin] in here." Therefore, he decided to seek a new life direction, one that would begin by never using heroin again. As it turned out, he never did.

Part of his epiphany was likely related to the fact that he was getting older and tiring of the prison routine. Further, during brief periods before this experience he had been exposed to 12-step programs that espouse complete abstinence from drugs and alcohol. It is certain, however, that his sudden realization that he would spend the majority of the rest of his life in prison if he did not change had a great impact on his thinking.

Family Damage. Diminishing family relationships greatly influenced Hippie and Junior. As well as attempting to maintain their drug habits, both men had spent most of their adult lives married to women who bore their children. When they made the decision to try to change by stopping their heroin use, both saw themselves as responsible for harms they were causing their wives and children. They felt remorseful and believed that if they did not alter their behavior they would lose their families. The following are illustrations of how they saw themselves within the context of their family relationships, and how certain situations and events that took place motivated them to change.

Long before the major turning point that steered him in another direction, Junior had come to see his heroin use as a problem. He married at age 21 and soon became a father. For years, he tried to maintain a loving relationship with his family. Supporting a drug habit and spending time in prison, however, hindered his efforts. He had already experienced one separation from his wife. She returned when he promised to quit using heroin. He was not able to fulfill that promise. The main thrust behind his eventual decision to make a real effort to change occurred when he reached his mid-30s. During this period, he came to see himself and his life as a heroin addict in such a negative fashion that he felt compelled to seek an alternative way of living. He clearly recognized the grave effects he was having on his family and felt that if he did not change, the damage he had already caused would only worsen.

A time came when Junior found himself confronted with two harsh realities. First, his wife, pregnant with his second child, was going to leave him again. This time she was threatening a legal divorce. "I loved her a lot and knew this was gonna be it," he told me. Second, friends of his (other heroin addicts) were coming to his house and referring to his 14-year-old son as "homeboy." He said, "I knew it was gonna corrupt my kid if he started looking up to these guys." He believed that being referred to as homeboy was a prelude to a future as an addict and a criminal and that, if nothing changed, "my son was gonna become like me." For the sake of his marriage and his son, Junior decided to make the effort to get clean by enrolling in a live-in drug program. "I did it to save my marriage. Plus my wife was pregnant—and so my kid wouldn't become a hype [heroin user]. I just knew that if I stopped sticking needles in my arm I wouldn't have to see my kid go through what I had to go through."

After leaving prison in his twenties, Hippie managed to become a successful businessman who got married and had a couple of kids. He smoked pot and used coke now and then, as did many of his successful friends. But heroin was something he detested. One day a friend came over and asked him if he wanted to smoke some opium. He said yes. As it turned out, it was black tar heroin. He told me that if the guy would have asked him if he wanted to smoke some heroin, he would have said, "Get the fuck outta' my house. 'Cause I had this image of heroin and junkies as no good." However, he thought smoking a little opium would be okay. He ended up loving it.

Over the next several months, Hippie became addicted and began his downward spiral that lasted for a couple of years. As well as having to hide his use of the drug, which made him feel guilty, and therefore in fear of retaliation or abandonment, he began to see himself differently because of his new associations and inability to stop. "I was pretty much, you know, a slave to the drug. I know I'm strung out. And I'm starting to cross lines that I would never have crossed. I'm associating with people that I just don't fuck with. And I'm fuckin' hatin' it."

His wife eventually caught him using and, after talking to her about his problem, he agreed to check himself into a treatment center. After several attempts at treatment, all of which failed, his wife told him, "I don't want you to come home. When you leave here I want you to move out." He was devastated. "I couldn't believe it. It was like I was down and somebody just came and started kicking me in my ribs. I was completely done. Demoralized as I could ever remember being. And I didn't know what I was going to do."

So Hippie ended up checking into the treatment facility again. Only this time he felt it was essential that he manage to kick his dope habit for good. Not only did he want his family back, he recognized the deplorable condition of his life. "I didn't get sober for me. I went in there to get sober to try to save my wife and two kids. I sort of didn't exist by that time. I was sort of this burnt out shell of a dopefiend that almost wasn't really even there." What he ended up learning about himself and his recovery though, was that he had to want to stay clean for himself, not for any other thing or any other person. Though his path was painful and difficult, it eventually took him where he wanted to be— back with his family. He summed up his experience by telling me that, "What I've found, the essence of the whole deal, is that I had to do all that stuff to get to a place where I was beat up enough to have a spiritual surrender so I could be transformed. I don't think it could have happened any other way."

New Arrests and Drug Treatment. In several cases, the fellas told me that a new arrest had a lot to do with their eventual commitment to change. In a way, it was like the straw that broke the camel's back. The new arrest left them in a position where they had a choice. They could either seek drug treatment or be sent back to prison. By this time, they were all near the end of their downward spiral. Jumbo, for example, told me that he was 51 at the time of his last arrest. Interestingly, it came in the form of a ticket. By then he had contracted diabetes, was not in good health generally, and was on probation with a prison suspended sentence for possession of heroin (that is, if he violated probation he could be sent to prison). He said one day he obtained some heroin and overdosed in his mother's bathroom. Afraid, because he had been in there for an extended amount of time and would not reply to her calls, she telephoned the police who came and broke down the bathroom door to determine his condition. He said when they found him, he was unconscious, "and the outfit [syringe] was still in my arm." He was taken to a hospital by paramedics and injected with an antidote. As soon as he was discovered to be an overdose victim, he was placed under arrest by a Chicano cop who decided, much to Jumbo's amazement, to give him a ticket at the hospital rather than take him to jail. He recalled the incident, "He gave me a ticket for under the influence. I never even heard of that."

Shocked with his luck, he left the hospital and started aimlessly walking down the street. He quickly realized that though he received only a ticket for his crime, it was still an arrest. That meant he would have to appear in front of a judge. Since he already had a suspended sentence, he would likely be sent back to prison. Try as he might, he could think of no way around his predicament. "I had no game plan, no con games, no lies left," he told me.

A few weeks later, he ran into a couple old friends. They told him they were in a live-in drug program and if he tried to get in and was accepted, it could keep him out of prison. The next day he went there and met the program director. He said the meeting was positive and encouraging. "We hit it off right away. He liked the old cons because they never made waves, never caused trouble unless they started using and then he'd kick them out." His application to enter was approved and he moved in the next day.

When he went to court, people from the program appeared on his behalf. They confirmed that he was making an effort to change and encouraged the judge to give him an opportunity at recovery. Their efforts may have had an impact. The judge told him he had "never seen anybody in his court so often" but was going to give him one more chance. He was given felony probation for his current charge, his prior probation was extended, and it was made clear that if he violated the conditions of his probation again he would go to prison. He said he could hardly believe his good fortune. "I was in shock. I was convinced that I was headed back to the joint."

He was impressed by what he had been seeing at the drug program and overwhelmed at how much influence it had with the court. On the way back to the program, he decided to give recovery a chance. He remembered thinking, "I'm gonna give this a real try. If they can keep me outta' prison and jail I'm gonna give it a try." As it turned out, he managed to stay clean for many years.

After years of struggle and often many failed attempts to turn their lives around, many of the fellas were finally able to make a sincere, conscious effort to find a new way to live. What they did to bring about this change is the topic of the next chapter.

6

Ways Out: Developing New Perspectives

An individual's incentive to seek a new way of living can occur because of unexpected contingencies or situations. In addition, the motivation for chronic addicts to change usually involves getting older, tired, and experiencing some form of bottom. A difficult question to answer, though, once we realize we would like to alter our lifestyles, is what is it we can actually do? What pathways exist that might help? The answer, of course, depends on who we are talking about. When it comes to people with backgrounds like the fellas, the idea of "getting clean" and staying out of prison by finding help in 12-step programs like Narcotics Anonymous is one viable, well-known course of action. As the story about the origins of NA indicated, it has not always been this way. Widespread knowledge that some addicts actually do get clean is a relatively recent phenomenon.

By 1987, I was 35 years old. At that time I had been incarcerated for about three years straight, had been using heroin and going in and out of prison for roughly 20 years altogether, and *had never once heard about an addict like me getting clean* and turning his life around. What I consistently *did* see were guys I knew, all addicts, coming back to prison after being out for fairly brief periods. They would leave the institution healthy and return looking "sucked up" or, in other words, skinny, sickly, and malnourished because not long after being released they reverted to their old lifestyles, which included the every-day use of drugs like heroin, cocaine, methamphetamine, and alcohol. I also heard about men getting out and dying. Some overdosed. Others got killed in violent confrontations. Finally, many who were released came back with sentences that were so long they would be impossible to complete.

Then one day, as I was hanging out with several friends in the yard, somebody mentioned that Zeke, one of the many guys who kept coming in and out for heroin-related charges, had been gone for quite awhile. In fact, he had not been returned to the prison in more than 18 months. Not only that, it was said that he was "doing good." This news was startling and almost unbelievable. How could he stay out so long? Had he turned into a snitch or something?[1] The person telling us about him said that he was staying clean by going to Narcotics Anonymous meetings. As well as being clean, we heard that he was living with a woman and working successfully as a car salesman. This was the first story I ever heard about anyone I could identify with really getting clean. It was also the first time I ever heard about Narcotics Anonymous. For the first time in my life I was at least aware of the possibility of a new life direction, and a place where people like myself get together on the outside to help each other improve their life situations.

MAKING THE CHANGE

People who undergo a radical shift in the way they see themselves and the world are often said to have undergone a process of conversion (Shibutani, 1991). Common examples include individuals who turn into revolutionaries because they get politically radicalized, or those who become religious zealots after getting "born again." To varying degrees, this process is what helped the fellas leave behind their old lifestyles and develop new self-concepts. The underlying effect of their exposure to, and interactions with, people in drug treatment and 12-step programs provided them with new reference groups and perspectives.

In most cases, the process of conversion takes considerable amounts of time (Athens, 1995; Shibutani, 1991). People prone to conversion are generally full of guilt, living unfulfilled lives, and have low self-worth. They are, therefore, receptive to new ideas and have an easy time rejecting their pasts. The change occurs from being assimilated into a different social world complete with new communication channels, meanings, and standards of behavior. Acceptance into the new group restores or helps build self-worth. The new meanings and self-concepts that follow are continually reinforced by new significant others, which are individuals who make up the audience whose judgements are most influential (Shibutani, 1991, 339). When an individual takes on the view of a new reference group—that is, his frame of reference for making observations learned in a new social world—he tries to live up to its standards. If the new perspective continues to provide relief, a lasting change may occur.

---

[1] Snitches, or informants, are often allowed to remain free from arrest, despite their drug use, as long as they provide police with information that can lead to the arrests of others.

Being motivated to change was an important component in the lives of the fellas. Before such a change could happen, however, they had to know that living differently was possible. This chapter examines some of the situations and events that exposed the fellas to the idea that making an effort to become involved in 12-step programs might be worthwhile. Next, after providing a brief overview of 12-step programs, we examine the processes of their conversion from the day they quit using drugs and alcohol until the time of the interviews. The focus is on what they actually did to make the conversion possible, obstacles they faced, and the effects this had on their self-evaluations and behavior.

Signposts

Of interest in this section is the manner in which the fellas were exposed to the idea that some addicts quit using drugs to pursue different lifestyles. Attention is given to some of the directions, or signposts, that led them to believe that participating in drug treatment or 12-step programs might be a worthwhile course of action.

Twelve-step meetings are available to prisoners in most penal institutions. In fact, they "are the only form of 'therapeutic support' offered in many prisons" (Maruna, 2001, 112). Their accessibility is widely publicized by guards. Most people behind bars know about the opportunity to attend meetings, yet few actually do. However, several of the fellas said they went to their first 12-step meeting while they were incarcerated. A few went because free coffee was offered, others because they heard women from the outside would be there. Winky said the main reason he went was to get out of his cell. At the time (1960s), he was president of a writing club that gave him the opportunity to interact occasionally with college students from the University of California–Davis who would visit from the outside. The students, part of a larger social movement that focused on rehabilitation, would meet with convicts to help them with their writing skills. Club leaders would place prisoner names on special lists. These lists would be given to, and approved by, guards who would use them to release the appropriate men from their cells during the time of the activity. To let prisoners know they were approved to participate, passes known as "ducats" would be sent to their cells indicating the day, time, and location of the event they would be attending. When that time came, a guard would open the cell and the prisoner could go to the activity. For California prisoners, a "ducat" is a pass out of the cell—a kind of get-out-of-jail-free card. Another convict who headed the prison AA group heard about Winky's position as leader of the writing club and approached him with a bargain. For putting his name on the list of prisoners who got out of their cells to go to the writers club meeting, he would be put on the list to get out of his cell to go to AA. Winky summarized the arrangement, "He said get me ducated to your deal and I'll get you ducated to mine." The plan worked, and Winky soon attended his first AA meeting.

Jumbo claimed to have gone to AA out of a sincere desire to better himself. After being incarcerated for two years, by 1964 he was immersed in a pattern of doing his time by taking advantage of every rehabilitation related activity the prison had to offer. He went to school, learned how to read and write, exercised regularly, and attended AA meetings. He also took on a variety of leadership roles. "I was chairman of the inmate council, president of AA [and] captain of the handball team," he proudly recalled. Though none of these men would get clean for many years, a signpost pointing to AA, NA, or both revealed itself in prison.

Most said they knew about 12-step programs from being in prison but just never attended meetings because of a lack of interest. Pelon told me, "AA's always been in the pens. I just never wanted to go." Bird said his first real exposure to recovery came from meeting a few people in jail who had tried, but failed, to get clean by going to NA meetings. So, he said, along with all the other conversations going on behind bars, "you'd hear a little of that stuff." More than just knowing AA or NA was there, talk about recovery seems to have become at least some portion of the dialogue going on between prisoners by the 1980s. This is not surprising since these were the same years that the "War on Drugs" resulted in more and longer terms of imprisonment for drug law violators (Baum, 1996), some of which had undoubtedly been exposed to drug treatment programs.

Several of the fellas' first encounters with anything related to 12-step programs were completely unexpected. It was often related to someone they knew who got clean and sober. Doctor Dee, for example, told me about a time when he had just been released from the central California prison at Soledad with a check for $1500. After getting back to the Los Angeles area, he called a homeboy of his who he described as "a guy I shot dope with for 20 years." He told him that he had just gotten out and had enough money for both of them to get loaded but needed a ride to cop (to cop means to buy or obtain narcotics). His friend said he would not be able to help because he was a sober member of AA. Not knowing what that meant, Doctor Dee responded, "That's bitchin', man. Come get me. You can be sober in AA tomorrow." After being told once more that being in AA made his request impossible, Doctor Dee hung up and called somebody else. The encounter was brief and seemingly trivial, but it exposed him to the idea that addicts really do quit using heroin by participating in 12-step programs. It took many more years of a downward spiral before he got clean himself. Yet that phone call gave him some hope and a sense of direction later in his life. He thought that if his old friend, who he saw as a chronic addict, was staying clean, maybe he could too. "When that guy wouldn't come to get me, it somehow must of registered in my mind. This was a guy that'd ride a bike with two flat tires in a hurricane 20 city blocks to get a shot of dope."

All the fellas told me they went to meetings at some point in their lives long before they got clean themselves. Wheels said he went to NA meetings in the San Fernando Valley back in the 1950s "when I was just a young punk." He went because it was a place to hide and feel safe. He remembered being impressed by seeing the words "we care" written across a sign attached to a podium at the meetings. During the interview, he recalled thinking at times of many individuals he met along his journey who were steering him toward an alternative course:

> It's like there have been people that have been signposts in my life. They've always been pointing me in the right direction. A lot of the time they didn't register. I didn't do anything with them then, but they were there, and I think they helped me along the way.

Without the signposts pointing them toward a different direction, the fellas might not have been able to turn their lives around. The whereabouts of new roads have to be known before they can be traveled.

THE TWELVE-STEP PROGRAM

Most of the fellas defined themselves as recovering addicts, or alcoholics, or both at the time of the interviews.[2] With the exception of Junior, whose conversion was related to religion and a strong church affiliation, their participation in 12-step programs was instrumental in helping them develop their new perspectives. As a result of interactions with other recovering people, they had gone through, or were in the process of, being delabeled as addicts and convicts, and relabeled as men in recovery (Trice and Roman, 1978). This redefinition of self is at the core of 12-step programs. What follows is an overview of the 12-step program and the processes that helped them change.

Program Overview

Twelve-step programs, which have been greatly influenced by the tenets of Christianity, can be seen as a form of Durkheimian religion characterized by mechanical solidarity. Like primitive societies that had little division of labor and great uniformity among their populations, the "glue" or bond that keeps them together is the perceived sameness or similarity of their members. Twelve-step groups resemble clans in traditional cultures. Members are attracted to the program and come to depend on each other because of their shared backgrounds and experiences. Just as clans often looked to physical objects like totems as spiritual guides and symbols of God, people in 12-step programs are encouraged to believe in a "Higher Power." Though this Higher Power is not specifically defined and is open to individual interpretation, it is a crucial program component shared by most participants. Like Durkheim's "collective conscience," which represented the collective identities, thoughts, norms, and values of traditional cultures, and was beyond the ability of any individual to change, 12-step programs are regulated by what members call a "group conscience." When it comes to making decisions that affect the group as a whole, the group conscience is the ultimate authority (Trevino, 1992).

---

[2] Exceptions were men who had been clean for a short period, usually less than three months.

Social homogeneity in 12-step programs, which have no experts or professionals with different status levels, is fostered in different ways. A process of self-labeling occurs when members refer to themselves as addicts or alcoholics before they speak at meetings. They strongly identify with each other because of their shared problem—alcoholism or addiction—and their shared goal—sobriety or clean time. Unity is further promoted from the distinct language[3] that has arisen from the beliefs and rituals of the program (Trevino, 1992). Many 12-steppers, in fact, come to see other members as their family. I often hear people in a meeting begin their turn at speaking by saying, for example, "Hi family. My name is Mitch. I'm an addict."

Twelve-step programs revolve around regularly attended meetings, which are generally held in schools, hospitals, or churches. There are two basic types of meetings. Most are participatory, that is, members take turns talking about their lives. There are also speaker meetings, which consist of one main speaker who talks for an extended length of time in front of the group. Twelve-step meetings are to participants what church is to the religiously oriented. Meetings are where individuals are exposed to the core 12-step ideology, which is communicated by reading segments of program related books.[4] These books, and the meaning of what they say, are like bibles for 12-steppers. Group members often refer to them as the "templates of recovery."

The program doctrine, as defined by the readings that take place at each meeting, states that addiction or alcoholism is an incurable, potentially fatal disease. This is why 12-steppers continue to define themselves as addicts and alcoholics. The doctrine holds that the only chance for a reprieve from this illness is to remain abstinent from drugs and alcohol, attend meetings regularly, and work the 12 steps, which help decrease a sense of individual uniqueness, self-centeredness, or egoism. In addition, becoming connected to the group is greatly encouraged.

After the material from the books is read, group members "share," or tell stories about themselves, their lives, and how they manage to stay clean and sober. Criticism of individuals in meetings is informally forbidden. Knowing they will not be condemned helps participants feel safe and welcome. Through the process of storytelling, members are able to gain a sense of shared identification with one another and also rethink or recreate their life history in such a way that they begin to see themselves as worthwhile human beings living meaningful lives. "This reworking of one's self-story according to the AA [or NA] model is itself the recovery process used in 12-step programs" (Maruna, 2001, 113).

---

[3] Sorting out the meaning of 12-step related language can be confusing. This has to do with differences in the language used in AA and NA. Many people go to either AA or NA. Some go to both. In AA, the focus is on alcohol. The amount of time one has successfully gone without a drink is called sobriety. In NA, the focus is on all drugs and alcohol. Lengths of abstinence in NA are called clean time. The general term used by insiders to define either or both groups together is "the program."

[4] In AA, they use the Alcoholics Anonymous "big book" (Alcoholics Anonymous, 1976). In NA, they use what is called the Narcotics Anonymous basic text (Narcotics Anonymous, 1982). For more about AA, see Denzin (1987, 1987a). For more about NA, see Peyrot (1985).

At some point during a meeting, individuals are recognized for remaining abstinent from drugs and alcohol for various lengths of time. They are given "chips" or "key tags" in their early recovery and birthday cakes every year thereafter. In this manner, the group expresses its approval for the accomplishment of "clean time" or "sobriety." This ritual, as well as validating people for their efforts, positively reinforces the value of staying clean and sober. It also gives new members a feeling of being included within the group.

Helping others, another manner of promoting inclusion, is a major component of 12-step ideology. Ways of helping include lending a hand to newcomers and "being of service" by getting involved with program-related duties. Because 12-step programs are not affiliated with any outside agencies, they depend on people sharing the responsibilities that allow functions such as meetings to take place. Members often "become of service" by volunteering their time and efforts for the benefit of the group. Examples of service-related duties, referred to as "commitments," include making coffee, setting up chairs, or being the temporary leader of a group. The necessary fees for meeting space and costs of other program related material such as literature and key tags comes from donations collected at each meeting by a treasurer.

Beneath the Meetings, Readings, and Dogma:
Honesty, Pain, and Humor

As well as helping me stay clean, people in 12-step programs have been instrumental in teaching me how to live a relatively "normal" life. Naturally, I have also been affected by family, friends, teachers, and opportunities that came my way. But, it seems to me, it was my ongoing relationships and activities associated with other recovering addicts, especially the first few years after being released from prison, that had the most influence.

Perhaps the most significant thing I've learned is that it's not so much what I'm doing (such as job or marriage) but how I'm doing it that best defines the quality of my life. How do I treat people? What are my motives and how much are they related to my selfish interests? Do I make the world a better place? How am I living today compared with last year, or 10 years ago? How do I hope to be living tomorrow? In 12-step programs, we learn that our chances of staying clean are enhanced when we work on improving ourselves by becoming better human beings.

Part of the attraction to meetings is that they are places where people often exhibit human emotions and feelings that are usually hidden from others. Frequently, they expose their deepest fears and pain. Recently, I heard a woman tell how guilty she felt because she couldn't stand her five children. Crying openly, she talked in an almost shrieking voice about how she never cared for them properly when she was hooked on crack cocaine. Now that she was clean, she didn't know how to handle them without flipping out all the time. They were driving her so crazy, she said, that she had to send them to a relative's house for awhile so she could work on getting herself together. Once, in the basement of a church located in a poor, urban neighborhood, I heard two women express the pain they were living with because their sons had been killed. Both sons had been shot, one by a cop, the other by a youngster from the neighborhood. Again and again, I've seen "newcomers," people attending a meeting for the first time, come in "tore up from the floor up." These people, if they are there because they are truly seeking help, tend to be in really bad shape because they are somewhere near their bottoms. One guy, toward the end of a meeting, introduced himself and then shamelessly asked, "I've stayed clean all day today. *But what am I supposed to do tomorrow?"* As tears flowed down his face he told us how he'd been using steadily for 30 years, had never been clean for more than a week, was losing his marriage, had already been fired from his job, and had kids who wouldn't talk to him because of his behavior over the years. There were many answers to his question. Among them were, "Keep coming back (to meetings)." "You're in the right place." "We love you." When people get brutally honest like that, something magical seems to happen. Perhaps by identifying with the pain and feeling empathy for the suffering person, everyone in the room is healing.

Meetings often are also loaded with humor that can diffuse tension and be cathartic. Frequently, people use self-mockery, which helps neutralize stigma and strengthen social bonds, by recounting grave situations from the past in a humorous manner (Terry, 1997). Recently, I took notes at a speaker meeting to capture the laughter I knew would be forthcoming. Here is a snapshot of what was said:

> I've been to 17 treatment centers and I learned the same in the last as I did in the first—I can't use nothin' [drugs and alcohol]. That shit turned me into a straight up hobo, pickin' up cans and butts off the street. Nose runnin', diarrhea, I mean sick. Drinkin' Mad Dog [cheap red wine] to get better, and shittin' all over myself. Took a TV to the pawn shop one time—on the bus—get it there and the guy says, "Man, this thing's not worth nothin'. It's so old it's got tubes."

> Treatment centers were a safe place to be. I'd always be there after spending my social security check, or after Christmas. Hell, that way I didn't have to get nobody no presents. After 9 months clean I realized a few things. Eating had become a habit. I noticed I was also washin' my behind.

On another occasion, a guy named Arty told about a particularly bad day. He was so sick from withdrawals, he said, that he attempted to rob a Seven Eleven store. Now, Arty didn't look like an armed robber, either. After entering the store, he tried the old stick-a-finger-through-the-pocket-of-the-jacket-trick, because he didn't have a gun, and told the person behind the counter that he was sticking the place up. Much to his chagrin, the guy didn't take him seriously and told him, laughing, to get the hell out of there. So then, Arty continued, he tried to rob *another* Seven Eleven store. This time he succeeded and made $20. Unfortunately, his dealer was nowhere to be found. Unable to wait, he attempted to purchase some heroin from a person on a street corner *and got burned for his money.*

This brief description of the 12-step program provides some backdrop for much of what follows. Except for Junior, the fellas stepped into this social world when they began making an effort to turn their lives around. To varying degrees, the ideas and people from 12-step programs became their new reference group. As such, it greatly affected their conversions.

Common Difficulties in Early Recovery

The difficulties the fellas had in their early periods of recovery had a lot to do with the perspectives they brought with them into the program. Their judgement of others, based on the standards common to the yard, made "fitting in" difficult. Several mentioned that when they first started coming to meetings they felt critical and antagonistic toward people in the group. One problem they mentioned was a deep-rooted aversion toward anyone in a meeting who would prescribe their personal version of the necessary rules or requirements for staying clean. Pelon described one of these so-called expert "twelve-stepologists." "You know, the guy who is always telling everyone how do it. That if you don't do the steps you'll die. Things like that."

Their assimilation into this new social world was often hindered because they tended to see themselves as superior to other group members. Many saw 12-steppers as weak and untrustworthy. As Shasta said, "I saw most of them as lames, weak punks and snivelers." In contrast, they typically viewed themselves as *real* addicts. Bird, for example, recalled the way he compared himself with others in the group when he first got clean. "They didn't use the drugs I did. If they did use the drugs I did, they didn't use them the same way and they didn't use them as long and, you know, they were different. I was always different. I shot more, longer, harder, better, faster, higher . . . all that."

Taking Action: Becoming Involved
in a New Social World

Regardless of how desperate a person is to change by trying to recover the 12-step way, it seems safe to say that the program needs to have enough of an appeal to encourage participation. The comraderie seen among old-time members at meetings is often perceived as one such attraction. Another is the kind and gentle way newcomers are welcomed. Perhaps most of all there is an atmosphere, as there may have been among clan members of traditional cultures, of genuine caring within the groups. Winky told me about something that attracted him as a newcomer roughly 16 years ago. When he walked into his first meeting, he was homeless, hopeless, sick, broke, and had no place else to go. Sensing that he was really at the bottom and struggling to survive, someone told him to take it easy and give himself a break—that it was going to be all right. His interpretation of this simple statement gave him immediate relief. "He told me that and it was like 'whew,'" he recalled. Huero, a relative newcomer to the program who seemed deathly afraid of using heroin anymore at the time of the interview, said he felt safe in meetings. "I know if I'm at that meeting there's not gonna be somebody sitting there going, 'Hey, let's go fix in the bathroom.'"

The fellas often mentioned experiencing a sense of relief and connection with the group after seeing and hearing someone use the language of the prison in a meeting. Although most 12-steppers were not ex-convicts, the few who were provided a means of identification and hope. Shasta told me that during his initial exposure to meetings he experienced a great deal of inner conflict because he felt so out of place. He felt his mere presence there implied he was admitting he had a problem. This, in turn, meant he was seeking help, an act that would be seen as weakness by a convict. Then one day in a meeting he heard another person, a former prisoner like himself, help relieve his turmoil by talking about how he did not care what anybody thought, he was there to save his life. "I could tell he didn't give a fuck what anyone thought about him—about what he was doing today," he remembered. His relief was strengthened when the individual made another statement that was convict inclusive. "Then he said if you're a fuckin' dopefiend or a convict this [the 12-step program] might help you."

In general, the fellas became involved in 12-step groups early in their recovery by attending many meetings and making new associations within the program. Winky said that the only time he was not at a meeting the first several months after he got clean and sober was when he was working or at a Salvation Army drug treatment program where he lived:

> I went to meetings all the time. I lived at the Sally [Salvation Army]. Any time I wasn't working or at that residence I was at a meeting. In those days you could go to morning meetings, a nooner, evening meetings, late night meetings. Went to 4 or 5 meetings a day on weekends.

Meetings were not the only means of developing their new perspectives. The fellas also got sponsors—people who act as guides through the steps, talked to other addicts on the phone, asked for and gave others rides to meetings, met with members in public restaurants for coffee, and became willing to pray. In other words, they gradually began to make connections and identify with people from the program. Sometimes their ideas about themselves and the world changed simply by listening to what was being said by others from the group. Pelon, for example, told me about how, while he was involved in a drug program during his last period of incarceration, people from outside NA groups would bring meetings to the jail. As time passed and he made an effort to hear what they were saying, he began to believe that he might actually be able to quit using heroin and live a better life. He remembered, "I'd hear their stories and start identifying a little more and a little more. I started thinking maybe it's not impossible for me to go out there and get a job and stay clean and feel good about myself." Without the willingness to listen, it would have been impossible for him to reap any benefit from what was being said. Without the chance to hear the stories, there would have been no opportunity for him to listen.

According to 12-step doctrine, old ways of thinking need to be relinquished. A statement often heard in meetings is, "It was our own best thinking that got us here." In other words, "our own best thinking" took us to our bottoms. This is partly why 12-step program ideology suggests the need to surrender one's will and life over to a Higher Power. "Although many members consider a Higher Power synonymous with the traditional conception of the deity of revealed religion—many others simply regard their own AA [or NA] group as God" (Trevino, 1992, 189). The main idea is to become open to new perspectives, especially those consistent with the doctrine of the program, which emphasizes the need to relinquish self-centeredness. During the interviews, the fellas repeatedly mentioned how they had been affected by the idea of "surrendering."[5] Huero, for example, who came to meetings intermittently for years but was never able to stay clean for long, told me that his sincere desire to change this time had to do with the fact that he had really given up all his old ideas. "I finally fucking surrendered," he said. Surrendering is difficult for a convict, however, because doing so is not consistent with a self-concept that revolves around projecting fearlessness. He mentioned that during his prior attempts at recovery, the notion of surrendering anything never carried much weight because he saw it as a sign of weakness. He said, "Before it was fuck you. That ain't me. I ain't no punk. Surrender this. Lock me up or do whatever you wanna do. I don't give a fuck." Yet the depths of despair and poor self-image he brought with him this time enhanced his willingness to try it. When he did, it seemed to provide relief. He remembered, "It was like a 100-pound weight was lifted off me. And I don't even know who I surrendered to. I just said, fuck it, I'm gonna do it somebody else's way." Bigwood, who also failed after making several efforts to get clean, said that he knew it was going to be different this time because he had finally surrendered. "There was just no more fight in me this time. I knew I was done and was willing to do whatever it took to stay sober."

Praying, which is a fundamental step-related action, is also something that surfaced during the interviews. Pelon, for instance, told me how his sponsor encouraged him to get on his knees to pray in the morning and ask his Higher Power to help him stay clean that day. At night, he was told it was good to pray again, only this time express gratitude for another day clean. He recalled his sponsor's words, "He told me, 'Hit the floor, man. Get on your knees. You gotta try this stuff. If you don't try it, how's it gonna work?'" Praying seemed foreign and strange. However, he took the advice and, over time, it became a regular part of his daily routine as it is for countless other 12-steppers.

Another action that aided the fellas' transition into this new social world had to do with the program rituals of taking cakes during meetings for being clean and sober for various numbers of years and making amends to people they had harmed. Vardo told me he had almost a year clean and sober by the time he was released from prison. During that year, he had become active in AA by attending meetings and working steps with an outside sponsor. On his

---

[5] The concept of surrender is a fundamental premise of the first step. In the basic text of NA, it is simply defined as "not having to fight anymore" (*Narcotics Anonymous*, 1982, 22).

first night out, he went to a meeting where he was given a cake to celebrate his first year of sobriety. Along with everyone else in the room, his Mom (who had been in AA for years) and several other family members were in attendance. Before he received the cake, one of his young nephews asked Vardo if he was scared to get up there in front of all those people. Protecting his convict image, he said no. "I ain't scared of shit, man. I've been in some of the worst yards [prisons] there are." Yet, when the time came to take the cake, he was riddled with fear. "All I could tell them was my name and that I'm an alcoholic. I was literally shaking." That same evening, he took his mother to a quiet room in a church and made amends to her for all the harm and pain he caused her during his life. "And we cried and cried over that," he recalled.

A majority of the men, especially those with substantial lengths of clean time, talked about the importance of being involved with and obligated to program-related activities. Winky explained how commitments had been a mainstay of his recovery since he first got sober. "I took commitments all over the place. Sweeping and mopping floors, making coffee, secretary of meetings. I've always stayed committed. I'd even start meetings if I didn't have something to do. Because that kept me involved." Doctor Dee said he basically surrounds himself with AA-related activities and associations who have become the new significant others in his life. "Currently, I'm secretary of the largest meeting in AA. I go to 3 or 4 meetings a week, have commitments— go to all the weddings and birthday parties. Everyone I socialize with is in AA." Like members of a clan in a traditional culture, these men never stray far from other "family" members.

While listening to the fellas' stories, I realized that becoming assimilated into the social world of the 12-step program seemed to be particularly hard for those who appeared to have become the most prisonized. Shasta, for example, told me about how hard it was for him to get to the point where he really felt like he belonged. After about a year into his recovery, he attended an NA convention that was held in a large hotel. These are gatherings of recovering addicts, usually numbering in the hundreds or thousands, who spend a weekend somewhere together celebrating their new lives. Convention activities include a great deal of socialization, meetings, dances, comedy shows, eating in fancy restaurants, coffee drinking, and cigarette smoking. His experience there had a lasting impact. It was the first time he saw so many NA members in one place having such a good time. "I was overwhelmed by all the dopefiends—hundreds and hundreds of dopefiends—partying, feasting, drinking sodas, coffee, chasing women, going to meetings." He also met other Chicanos who had been to prison. Their presence and the way they welcomed him reminded him of past associations, helped him feel more comfortable, and reinforced the idea that his participation in the program was a worthwhile endeavor. He remembered how they helped him feel included. "I'm meeting these old tecatos [old heroin addicts] who had years in recovery. And I'm hearing, 'Hey homes, how's it going? Welcome. Hope you stick around.'" His sense of not belonging stemmed from him seeing himself as different than most others at meetings. This sense of alienation was related, in part, to him almost acting out violently against group members on more than one occasion. Help eventually came from three men who understood what he was going through. They were individuals he could relate to and trust. After meetings, they would take him out for coffee (a common after meeting activity) and talk to him about his life and the program. He remembered them telling him he needed to communicate more with people he felt comfortable with and, meanwhile, not hurt members he saw as different:

> They'd tell me, "Fuck all these lames. It ain't about them. It's about you doing what you gotta do for you. And that means use the fucking phone. Get some fucking numbers. Go up to dudes and introduce yourself."
> They said, "Just don't do anything stupid. Don't hit anybody."

Importantly, those who had difficulty assimilating were accepted into the group regardless of their backgrounds or perspectives. The program, like the social worlds of the oppositional cultures from which they came, was a place where it was okay to be a convict or a regular. They were not regarded as "bad." They were not only accepted but welcomed just as they were. This helped them stay around long enough to be able to identify with, talk, and listen to people they perceived to be like themselves. This, in turn, aided them in overcoming the hurdles they faced and continue their assimilation into this new social world.

Perceived Effects of Program Affiliated Actions

Most of the fellas, especially the ones with lengthy amounts of clean time, attributed the fact that they quit using drugs and alcohol directly to their involvement with 12-step programs. Weasel, for example, said that his association with NA was the only thing that ever worked to keep him clean. "I'd been searching for any answer I could find that would help me quit for a long time. But I never found one that would help me stop until I started going to NA." Several told me that if it were not for the actions they had taken as members of a 12-step program, they doubted if they would still be alive. I often heard them say, for example, "AA [or NA, or the program] saved my life."

The men often referred to benefits they had gained by becoming active in the 12-step social world. Pelon mentioned that meetings "helped him learn simple things that everyone should know." These "things" included learning that everyone struggles in their lives, understanding different ways of interacting with others, and appreciating the value of being honest. Shasta talked about the relationship he had with his sponsor early in his recovery. He said that, more than anything else, the man gave him the sense of being appreciated. "This guy made me feel like I was somebody that I never thought about before. He made me feel welcome—like I was an actual asset to his life." Kickstand said that one of the major effects of the relationships he had with people in the program were that they made him think about himself in ways that never crossed his mind before. "They've helped me think about where I've been and where I'm going. And that I'm not the only one doing this thing."

Program participation often cultivates beliefs in spirituality, a subject most of the fellas mentioned during the interviews. In meetings, spirituality is often related to individual conceptions of a Higher Power and ideas that include being honest, helping others, letting go of individually derived, self-centered ways of thinking, and situating oneself within a larger social context (Peteet, 1993). Bozo attributed the way he feels about others to the level of spirituality he has developed since getting clean. He said that before his involvement with NA, he would see people suffering, as in an earthquake or a flood on television, and think "better them than me." In contrast, when he is exposed to such dramatic devastation or any type of human pain today, he feels compelled to help. He explained what he meant: "Today I feel their pain. I have this spiritual piece that's connecting me with them. It makes me feel for them. It makes me want to go do something for them. That's what that spiritualness does to me." Hippie told me that he considers himself to be spiritually connected as long as he stays clean. "If I don't get loaded, I'm connected. It's that simple." He said that the relationships he has with others, an effect of his spirituality, are enhanced when he works the steps, goes to meetings, and helps newcomers. Junior, the only non–12-stepper who began his clean time by spending a year in a Christian-based drug program, said his education about spirituality since getting clean has helped him learn about humility. He claimed that changing his view of himself and the world was not easy because by the time he turned himself into the program he was 40 years old and very set in his ways. He resisted the ideas of others, be they family members, counselors, or friends who saw problems with his actions. "I always had my answer, my justification," he said. Being humble was difficult. It allowed no room for pride. His ability to experience the effects of humility, something he perceives to be directly related to the relationship he has with a Higher Power, came when he learned that all he had to do was keep quiet in the face of criticism. "I learned that when somebody corrected or admonished me because they thought I was wrong to keep my mouth closed. I learned to receive it. Hear it. How I learned to receive it was just by not saying anything." Though being humble is not something he is always able to do successfully, he continues making the effort to listen rather than argue. He seemed convinced that being humble improves the quality of his life because it takes away the need to fight and resist whatever seems to be opposing his own way of thinking. "Humility don't need the last word. Humility don't need to be right."

As the men's self-concepts changed, so did their general perception of others. They often mentioned that they felt more compassion and empathy for people than they did before. Several expressed sympathy for those they now see as being similar to themselves when they were using drugs or when they first got clean. Doctor Dee told me how he feels when he sees somebody who appears to be under the influence of heroin. "Today I feel sorry for them. What used to look cool looks pathetic. I thought I was the coolest fucking dude on the block when I was like that." He continued by saying he now sees people who act like he used to as stuck in their ways and pitiful. "I meet people who were just like I was. Their worldview is rock solid. And there is no argument that will change that. I see them now as unfortunate. They're uneducated and unwilling to see an alternate view."

Nearly all the men talked about how the value of helping others had taken on new meaning since they became involved in 12-step programs. In every NA meeting, we hear "we can only keep what we have by giving it away" read from the Basic Text. This is generally interpreted as meaning we can only stay clean and sober by helping other struggling addicts and alcoholics. We are taught that happiness comes from giving without wanting anything in return. Vardo told me he believes the very meaning of life is related to helping others. He said it gives him a sense of purpose and a great deal of personal fulfillment. "I really feel good when I'm helping other people. I really truly believe that that's what life's about. And I think that's what sobriety has given me more than anything."

Many of the ideas learned in 12-step programs, including the value of helping others, are transferred to the wider, outside world. The fellas often mentioned practicing program-related principles in their marriages, communities, or places of employment. Pelon mentioned that one of the ways he "gives back" is by helping homeless people he sees on the streets. "I give 'em food. I'm out there talking to them. I know they're feeling the pressures of the system and appreciate the help." Weasel said he learned the value of giving by being a member of NA. Now, after eight years clean, he makes regular efforts to help others in a variety of situations outside the program. For instance, he volunteers his time at a local television station and frequently makes trips to Mexico to help his family. Since getting clean, he became romantically involved with a woman. Eventually they had a child together. Though the relationship did not work out, he said, he still does what he can to help. "I'll send her about 50 or 60 a month to help. Let her know that if she needs any help and I can give it she can have it." Lending a hand to others can provide a deep sense of gratification and fulfillment.

NEW LABELS: REFERENCES
TO SELF IN RECOVERY

Several of the attributes the fellas used to define themselves had been developed since they quit using drugs and alcohol. Some were made in reference to their affiliation with 12-step programs. As Hippie said, "I see myself as a recovering alcoholic, dopefiend, with the intention of being in recovery one day at a time for the rest of my life." Others had to do with things related to different areas of their lives, including their jobs, school, and interpersonal relationships. Wheels summed up his home life and occupation in a sentence. "I'm a house husband. I get up, get the kid off to school and do the chores around the house." Except for the few who had not been clean for long, the differences in the way they referred to themselves since getting clean and sober, compared with how they defined themselves at the end of their using and drinking careers, were dramatic.

The way the fellas characterized themselves often reflected mainstream values and their new perspectives as recovering people. Wheels, who felt he had been "banished from his tribe" in prison, mentioned a conversation he had with a parole officer after he was released from a treatment-oriented halfway house at the end of his prison sentence. The officer went into the usual lecture given to newly freed individuals about the conditions of parole, which include not using drugs, giving up the right to be protected from search and seizure violations by legal authorities, and the need to obey all laws. After patiently listening until the man was finished, Wheels recalled telling him, "You know what? All that doesn't really mean anything to me. I got a job. I'm going to NA meetings. I'm clean. I'm a responsible person." Rather than having to defend himself against the threat of the criminal justice system by lying about his drug use and other deviant activities, as he did in the past, he was able to list attributes about himself that are highly valued in the mainstream culture. Today he is still active in NA, volunteers his time at a prison to try to help prisoners improve their lives, is married, has a stepson, and works as a drug and alcohol counselor.

Doctor Dee defined himself using characteristics that would be seen as commendable by mainstream standards. He credited the change in his life and the way he sees himself primarily to AA but, unlike most of the other fellas, also recognized he has been influenced by wider social forces:

> I think not only by AA, but also the educational process I've gone through [has affected me]. This is my 5th year in school. My worldview has changed a lot. I've become more open minded. I came from the bushes and I'm about to graduate from UCSB. I'm a board member and officer of an environmental group.

Along with being a full-time student, he is also married, father of a young son, and works at a part-time job. In general, he seemed to exhibit a positive self-evaluation, something that would have been impossible when he lived in the bushes and panhandled money for wine.

Just as they did in prison, the regs had a tendency to view themselves as elites within the social world of recovery where their convict-like characters and illustrious backgrounds were often seen as admirable traits. The fact that they are "doing good," despite their pasts, is evidence for other members that anybody can "make it." Jumbo, for example, talked about how he was afforded a great deal of respect by other addicts in the program during his first year clean. "I was a leader there. I was an example. I was an old guy, an old hype [heroin user], an old ex-con and I'm doing it. Pretty soon everybody wanted me to speak in meetings. Everybody wanted me to be their sponsor." As time passed, he went to fewer and fewer meetings. He now works in a counseling center affiliated with the local police department that targets people who are drunk in public. Rather than take them to jail, the police bring them to his place of employment—a quasi-detox ward—and give them a chance to sober up. His job is to oversee their stay and, if they are willing, help them get into some kind of treatment program. He sees himself as an example and seems to maintain a high level of gratification from his efforts to help the downtrodden.

Several of the fellas made direct comparisons between the way they were before they got clean and the way they see themselves today. Some, especially those who seemed to have been the most prisonized, talked about how their tendency to think and react violently had declined since they had gotten clean. Shasta, for example, told me he was not as apprehensive and distrustful as he was when he first got into recovery more than five years ago and that he no longer feels as compelled to hurt others as he did back then:

> I'm not afraid of the way I think today as I was in those first couple of years. I was scared shitless. 'Cause the first thing that would cross my mind [in a situation he perceived as threatening involving another person] was—that fucking punk he just doesn't know [who I am—a fearless convict]. Well, I'm gonna show him. That was the first thing [I thought about back then]. Some retaliatory [type of] thinking.

Vardo said that the difference between what he was like before and what he is like now is unbelievable. "It's like night and day." Before getting involved in AA, he found himself spending most of his time in prison. His last conviction was for armed robbery. Currently, he works as a drug and alcohol program supervisor in a county jail, is married, and still active in AA. "I was hurting myself and other people before and today I'm trying to help myself and other people." As we spoke, he told me that his mother died since he has been clean. As hard as it was to see her go through the dying process, he felt good about himself because she was able to see him living a drug and alcohol free life before she passed away. During her illness, he was sent to a pharmacy to pick up some morphine that she was being given for pain. Keep in mind, this was a guy who had done armed robberies to get money for heroin, which has almost identical effects. The fact that he did not feel like using any of it surprises him to this day. It was a milestone in his recovery and evidence of his new perspective. He told me, "Before I would'a gone through a brick wall with a spoon to get that stuff. I would'a robbed my Mom for it. For some reason I didn't. My life is that much changed."

Something that surfaced repeatedly among the men who had been clean and sober for several years was their realization that they were not bad people. Winky, for example, claimed that since he quit drinking alcohol, his self-concept had improved a great deal. "If I had any opinion about myself when I first got sober it was negative," he said. It took several years before he saw himself as okay. He continued:

> By the time I took my 8-year cake I knew that I had a good side and a bad side. That I'm just a human being with all that entails. But I also believed by then that I was a good guy that deserves health, happiness [and] prosperity. That it's okay to have it. It's okay to be okay.

Today he no longer eats out of trash cans, begs for change, or sleeps wherever he happens to fall. With 16 years of sobriety, he works for AA's central office in his local community, pays his bills with money he legally earns, and does a lot to help others who are struggling. Bigwood, who had been clean for 13 months at the time of the interview, told me simply, "I'm learning I'm not a bad person."

Several of the fellas mentioned that one of the most positive effects of their process of recovery was coming to the realization that they are not, and need not aspire to be, seen as special in the eyes of others. They learned that many of the goals promoted by the mainstream culture are recipes for misery and feelings of inadequacy. Bozo recalled how, while doing the steps, he had a hard time looking at himself. He said it had been difficult to write down things he had done to hurt others throughout his life (4th step) and then openly acknowledge those actions with another human being (5th step). Yet, by doing so, he learned that his belief in the value of chasing material objects to look good to others was a mistake and did not lead to happiness. He said he also learned about his greed and selfishness:

> I always thought the more material things I had, the more people I had around me, the more luxury I had, the better it made me feel. Now I know that didn't work. Now I know I was just trying to be king of the hill. Today I'm trying to be just another addict in recovery.

Hippie told me that during his first few years of participating in AA, he took many commitments and did a lot to help other alcoholics and addicts. He said that back then, though, many of his efforts "to be of service" were made as an attempt to be seen as important by others in the program. Today, in contrast, he strives for anonymity and humility rather than self-glorification. "Now I like it when I feel like I'm just another Joe—just another guy. I'm just another sober guy. That's all." Similarly, Doctor Dee claimed that he has learned it is important for him to refrain from trying to be seen as unique. "I think a big part of sobriety for someone like me is humility—to be an Indian instead of a chief." For these men, caring for others and seeing oneself as "just another guy" seems to be a meaningful way of living. It indicates they have taken on the values of the 12-step culture, which discourages efforts to portray oneself as special. Indeed, when I asked Hippie what he hoped for in the future, he said, "More humility, more compassion and more tolerance for others. Really, I just wanna be a better human being." Such ideas and goals are uncommon and far removed from that which was valued in the bushes, shooting galleries, or cellblocks of their pasts. They may, in fact, be a step up from lifestyles and ways of thinking associated with many of us who embrace notions of specialness and a need to acquire more and more material commodities as a result of living in a consumer driven, market culture (Fromm, 1976).

7

Ↄ

Afterthoughts and a Brief Glimpse of the Fellas Three Years Later

This book is not meant to be something that advocates for the "War on Drugs" can point to and say, "These men got clean, so anybody with drug problems can do the same." That is simply not the case. Those of us with extensive histories of addiction and imprisonment who manage to turn our lives around are rare exceptions. We have been able to succeed despite the social structures that influenced us to use drugs in the first place and the many forces that often inhibit such change. In general, as our feelings of alienation within the mainstream culture decreased, the compassion, empathy and sense of connection we developed with others was given a chance to grow. Not everyone with similar backgrounds entertains the idea of change. Further, not everyone who manages to get clean stays clean.

EXCLUDED BUT NOT FORGOTTEN

As this project began to take shape, it became clear to me that I would need to find a group of guys like the fellas to interview. Based on the relationships I had with other NA members, I assumed that several of the men I knew who fit the criteria I was looking for would be more than willing to participate. Unfortunately, a few of those I was more or less counting on did not manage to stay clean until the interviews actually began. Though they were not included for that reason, what happened to them is worth mentioning because their fate (as did Marisol's in the beginning of the book) further illustrates the harsh effects of the "War on Drugs" and the difficulty of overcoming the effects of heroin addiction and imprisonment.

Two of the men I hoped to interview died. Arty (the same guy who got laughed at for trying to rob a Seven Eleven) had done one short stint in the California Department of Corrections for a drug-related charge, had been clean for three years, started using heroin again, got arrested for possession of a controlled substance, and was facing his second prison sentence. The last time I saw him was in a room adjacent to where an NA meeting was taking place in a church. He was by himself and clearly miserable. All I can remember him telling me is, "Damn brother. I just don't wanna go back [to prison]." Before three more days had passed, he committed suicide by jumping off a freeway overpass and landing on the windshield of a car traveling between 65 and 70 miles per hour. Though it is impossible to say exactly what motivated him to take his own life, we can speculate that he felt horrible about both his situation and himself. If it wasn't for the cultural stigma against addicts, the drug laws, and his exposure to 12-step ideology—all of which condemn drug use—Arty might still be with us today.

Another guy I mistakenly counted on was Bryan, who I saw come in and out of prison and NA meetings for several years. I also wrote him while he was doing time. In an article where I attempted to portray some of the damaging effects of imprisonment, I quoted an excerpt from a letter he sent me before his last parole board appearance about his fear of getting out:

> I have a lot more shit to trip on than the board. Like getting out. I was laying on my rack [bunk] this morning thinking about the streets, stomach in knots, palms all sweaty. I hate it here. But I'm also scared to get out. Don't know why bro, just makes me scared. Remember how you felt on the van riding to Chino [trip from jail to prison] or wherever? Well, that's how I feel when I'm about to get out. My guts all in a knot. Remember the last time I got out? You met me at Carrow's [restaurant]. Well, right before that at the greyhound station I felt like crying when I got off that bus. Not cause I was happy either. (Terry, 2000, 121)

After getting released, Bryan went to NA meetings and lived in a drug program run by the Salvation Army. I had hoped to interview him during this time. Like Arty, though, he began using heroin again. To avoid going back to prison for a parole violation, he left the state. Within two months, his murdered body was found outside Tucson, Arizona, in an area where homeless people find places to sleep in bushes to keep their presence hidden. Nobody knows what might have happened to him if addicts were seen and treated differently. For the most part, nobody seems to care. Deaths such as these are chalked up to the horrors of addiction. Wider social forces, including those of the criminal justice system, are virtually neglected. Rather than interview either Arty or Bryan, who grew up on the same block in a white, middle-class neighborhood and were friends since childhood, I attended their funerals.

Japo is a regular who has spent many years in prison, never for a violent crime. When I met him, he was 50 years old, had been clean for more than four years, and was an active member of 12-step programs and the community. One of his passions during this period was working with other ex-convicts to help youngsters who were involved in street gangs. Then he started using heroin again. Eventually, he was arrested after narcotics agents found less than a quarter gram of cocaine and heroin residue on a spoon that was used to cook the drug in the car he was driving. A woman who was riding with him that fateful day "cooperated" with police by informing them that he was the owner of the drugs that were discovered. Japo told me the cocaine belonged to her. After refusing an offer by the district attorney's office of 17 years for a guilty plea, he was convicted by a jury and sentenced to 32 years to life under California's "Three Strikes" law. Today, as Japo once again calls a prison cell home, he is seeking legal relief from the appellate courts.

THE FELLAS: THREE YEARS LATER

Three years have passed since I completed interviewing the fellas. To bring their stories up to date, I attempted to contact as many of them as possible to find out how they are doing today. Of those I was able to find, some were still doing good. Others were not as fortunate. I was able to find out something about some of these from others who knew of their situations. Part of what is told here, then, is what I heard from the grapevine.

Bozo, after leaving the area, left no trace of his whereabouts. Perhaps he went back to New York. Similarly, nobody I knew had heard about Wheels or Bird. Sticks was in Oregon counseling addicts while working on a master's degree. Bigwood relapsed not long after the interview. Today he is on a methadone maintenance program and struggling. Baggy relapsed as well. During the past three years, he has been in and out of drug programs. Currently, he is back at Hope House, the exact place he was living when he told me his life story, and clean again. Finally, I was told that Huero did not manage to stay clean long at all. Within 60 days of the interview he was in jail for a new charge and on his way back to prison.

Vardo helped me learn about Jumbo who relapsed after staying clean more than seven years. Shortly after Jumbo started using heroin again, he began living the life of a desperate addict. After losing his job and experiencing a quick downward spiral, and getting into a huge fight with his son (who was recovering from brain surgery) because Jumbo got caught stealing some of his son's opiate-based pain medication, he turned himself in to the same live-in program that helped him get clean the first time around. I talked to him on the phone there. After telling me the painful story of his relapse, he told me was back on track, clean again, and "doing the deal."

Wino managed to make it nearly three years before he started using again. I unexpectedly ran into him one day while visiting somebody else at Hope

House. Like Jumbo, he said his relapse took him "down" real fast. Within weeks, he was doing a 90-day stint in the county jail for an under-the-influence charge. While there, he took advantage of a drug and alcohol program offered within the minimum custody section of the facility. Before he was released, he applied and was accepted to the Hope House program. Last I heard he was still clean and doing good.

At this point in time, Brains is perhaps the worst "casualty" of all the fellas. After almost three years clean, he began taking prescription drugs to get high. Before long, the pill taking was supplemented by heroin injections. His relapse was especially painful for me because I had a close, personal relationship with him the entire time he was clean. He always had a positive outlook, regularly went out of his way to help people, knew a great deal about music, which is one of our shared interests, and was just great to be around. Not long after he started using drugs again, he called me on the phone to ask for money. I could barely understand him because his words were so slurred. Within the next year, he had spent several months in jail for being under the influence of narcotics. Since then, he has contacted me by mail on several occasions claiming he was homeless, in bad health, and in desperate need of money. Kickstand told me just the other day that he believes Brains has had several unnecessary surgeries on one of his shoulders for the single purpose of obtaining prescriptions drugs. Whether that is true or not is basically irrelevant. Suffice it to say that the man is really struggling. Someone from Hope House recently told me they saw him showing up "on the line" (the "line" of homeless people who show up there for free food and shelter) now and then and that he looks like a walking corpse. I hope that he will get to the point where he again seeks recovery. If he doesn't, I'm afraid he may die very soon.

Along with being married, Pelon is enrolled in a master's degree program and doing well in his academic endeavors. Junior is still married, exercises regularly, works every day in the construction business, and is still very involved in the church. After enduring a second round of chemotherapy (he had undergone the first shortly before our interview), Rabbit has been "cancer free" for more than three years. As well as remaining clean and sober, he switched occupations since the interview. Rather than cut hair, he now owns and operates his own truck and trailer. Last time I tried to call him, he and his wife were in Mexico on vacation. Hippie is still married, still running his cabinet-making business, which he said keeps him very busy, and still actively involved in the 12-step program. He continues to visit the jail once a week to talk to addicts and alcoholics who may not have heard the "message of recovery." Last time we talked, he was complaining about having to serve on jury duty.

Weasel is doing good. Now 63 years old, he has recently married and is the proud father of a two-year-old son. He admits that his marital relationship creates tension in his life, in part because his wife, who is 30 years old and white, and he come from such different backgrounds. Impatience, anger, and issues with money were a few of the "problems" he claimed to regularly encounter (welcome to the world, Weasel). At the same time, he acknowledges his own part in their conflicts and told me how they do their best to resolve them by communicating as openly as possible. All in all, he said, he was happy and felt like he was getting a second chance at life.

Winky is currently employed as the central office manager by the Alcoholics Anonymous organization of his local community—the same location he called when he was looking for his friend Bob just before getting sober more than 19 years ago. When I talked to him, he said he was taking interferon treatments, the current western medical solution for hepatitis C.[1] Though the virus had not advanced to the point where he is unable to work, he did say that he suffers from a lack of energy. Whether his symptoms are from the virus or the interferon, which typically has strong "side" effects, is unclear. All in all, he remains an active member of his recovery community.

Doctor Dee is actually learning about doctoring! He is currently a graduate student in the prestigious physician assistant program at Georgetown University in Washington, D.C. His wife, who is also in recovery, and their nine-year-old son, relocated with him from the West Coast. Their transition has gone well. He tells me they love it there. When I speak with him on the phone I can tell he is enthusiastically engaged in life, an active participant in the mainstream culture and, for the time being at least, a long way from the bushes he used to call home.

Shasta is still clean and remains very active in NA. He firmed up a relationship he has been in for several years by getting married last June. They live with her two sons. He has a job he enjoys at Home Depot, and whenever I talk to him, he expresses tremendous joy about the time he gets to spend with his grandchildren. His convict identity, which he continues to maintain to a certain degree, seems to contradict the warmth and love he conveys when he speaks about the gratitude he has for his new way of life.

Vardo and his wife are in the process of selling some property they bought a few years ago for a hefty profit. He still works as a drug and alcohol program supervisor at the local county jail, but may be leaving there when the sale of their home is complete. Though he enjoys working with addicts, the animosity and subsequent stress he receives from administrators and guards at that facility have taken their toll. As he has learned firsthand, "treatment" and incarceration are fundamentally contradictory because one is geared toward "helping," whereas the other revolves around "control" and "institutional security." Surfing remains his lifelong passion. He and his wife plan to travel extensively with the money they have made.

Kickstand is perhaps the biggest miracle of them all. This is a guy who used to tote sawed off shotguns into bars on his Harley Davidson motorcycle and express himself however he felt was necessary. Living without a gun was not an option. After spending roughly 25 years behind bars, he was very likely the most prisonized of all the fellas. Not only has he remained clean for more than 3 years now, but he also has not been in a single fight that entire time. He lives alone, regularly attends 12-step meetings, and is self-employed as a

---

[1] I have never met one person who has been an intravenous drug user who has not tested positive for hepatitis C.

welder. His evolvement as a recovering addict seems to mirror what I saw happen when I recently took him and three other NA members to my sister's house for a visit. My sister and her husband, a master sergeant in the Air Force, along with their five boys who range in age from 8 to 14, are fundamental Christians who live on a military base. None of these people had ever met before. For a good while after we got there, Kickstand was totally quiet. He later told me how awkward and out of place he felt when he first arrived. Eventually, though, he ran into my brother-in-law who was alone in the kitchen and struck up a conversation. "I couldn't believe it," he remembered. "I was so afraid that I wouldn't fit in around them people, them being so religious and all, and then when I got to talking to that dude I found out he ain't no different than anybody else. Hell, we were in there kickin' it like old friends. He's good people." After that, he began opening up to everyone who was there, including my 91-year-old grandmother. We even went outside and had a blast playing basketball with my nephews. The youngest seemed to affect him the most. He later told me, "That littlest one was really a trip. All you had to do was give him the fucking ball and he immediately got super happy."

SELF-CONCEPTS AND BEHAVIORAL CHANGE: A FINAL GLANCE

Like previous research about people leaving behind lives of crime (Irwin, 1970; Maruna, 1997, 2001; Shover, 1985) or addiction (Biernacki, 1986; Ronel, 1998; Vaillant, 1983), this book used the notion of a self-concept to explain changes in behavior. Given that some of the fellas began using heroin again, however, the validity of this relationship might be questioned. How can it be that during one period of time an individual's self-concept helped keep him off drugs, while in another it did not? The answer, I believe, is that a complete conversion tends to take a good deal of time (Athens, 1995; Shibutani, 1991). DiClemente (1994) argues that a lasting personality change can take between 7 and 10 years. The amount of time it takes will be highly variable and related to the entirety of circumstances, as well as to the way they are interpreted, in each person's life. For many, this process may never really end. When juxtaposing one's self-concept to behavioral change, it is plausible to assume that the longer one is able to maintain new, meaningful associations and activities, the more likely it will be that a regression will not take place.

A major reason that people like the fellas have such difficulty becoming assimilated into the mainstream culture is that the perspectives they learned in prison and the street, which are like ghosts from their pasts, haunt them. Defined elsewhere as "hangover identities" or "role residual," these ghosts are like leftovers from former reference groups that cloud and affect current roles (Ebaugh, 1988). As they attempt to become acceptable in the eyes of society, they judge themselves and their actions using criteria from two different social worlds, each with different demands. These demands, which cannot be satisfied, lead to a sense of confusion, guilt, and alienation because what is approved in one social world is condemned in the other (Shibutani, 1986, 313). The contradictory meanings derived from each affect current expectations, evaluations, and actions. Some examples will illustrate this dilemma.

Vardo recently told me that he had to remove two men from the drug program he oversees because their urine tests indicated they had recently used illegal drugs. Because of the program rules and their probation, this meant that they would be immediately sent to jail. He claimed it bothered him a great deal and made him "feel like a rat." As a drug and alcohol counselor, making critical judgements against people who test dirty for drugs is expected. Further, this action is demanded by his employer, a county sheriff's department. However, informing on others or cooperating with guards in any way that will bring harm to another prisoner, or "being a rat," is unacceptable in the prison culture. The exact same action means two different things, and how it is seen depends entirely on the frame of reference used to define the situation. In short, the feelings he had were the result of his self-evaluation, which differs depending on which reference group he uses to judge himself. As a counselor, what he did was expected and acceptable. Such an action for a convict could lead to complete ostracization by other prisoners. Though this man has been clean and sober for more than 10 years, he still has difficulties dealing with the contradictions between his old versus new reference groups—or his old and new self.

For the fellas, reintegration was often hindered by role residual. To this day, several still do not have checking accounts. Having never had one, and unable to grasp how one might make their lives easier, they pay cash for everything. This is understandable considering prisoners do not have such accounts and drug dealers are not known for accepting checks. Huero called me one day and told me he really felt like using heroin. Telephoning others is an action that people in 12-step programs are encouraged to take before they use a drug. The idea is that by talking to another recovering addict, the craving will pass. Later, he mentioned how hard that phone call was to make because asking for help seemed like a sign of weakness. It would have been if judged from a convict perspective. The men were especially haunted by situations in which they interpreted themselves as being disrespected by others. Such events took place everywhere from freeways to bookstores. Doctor Dee told me, "On the freeway I feel like I want a gun I get so pissed off. I try to be polite but I just can't stand being disrespected." Writing checks, telling on people, and expressing weakness do not fall within the norms of their prior social worlds. Getting "pissed off" and angry, on the other hand, was not only normal but expected.

Old behavioral patterns can return following increasing levels of isolation from one's new reference group and a general decline in well being. Jumbo, for example, attended meetings less and less over time and basically quit associating regularly with other recovering addicts. Then he was told he was no longer needed at his place of employment. Without another reference group and something else to do to fill the void left by the loss of his job, which he highly valued, he naturally fell back into his old, familiar ways.

Reverting to an old lifestyle can also be affected by experiencing extreme degrees of emotion. I once knew a mechanic who managed to stay clean for roughly eight months by becoming involved in NA. Blue, a former heroin addict and prisoner, had lived with the same woman for several years. He and his girlfriend, who had a two-year-old daughter, were known to have severe confrontations. One day, after a heated argument, Blue stormed out of his house and, in a rage, began aimlessly walking down the street. Later, he told me what happened:

> Man, I was so pissed off I couldn't see straight. And I just started walking. Along the way I saw a liquor store. Next thing I know, I'm thinking about a bottle of Night Train [cheap red wine]. This isn't easy to explain brother, but what happened next was so weird. It was like as I took the next step I changed. It was like as I took that step I left the skin of the new Blue, the recovering Blue, and stepped right back into the skin of the old me. And then it was like I'd never been clean, like nothing ever changed.

Blue didn't buy that Night Train. But he also didn't stay clean much longer. Within two months after he started using drugs again, he was back in jail facing charges for forgery.

Blue's words made sense to me. Sometimes, the old self can resurface in what seems like a flash. Once, after being clean for four or five years, I stopped for gas on a hot, summer day in the San Fernando Valley. As I pulled into the station, I noticed someone using a public phone located on the property. Immediately, I sized the guy up as being an addict. Not only that, I somehow felt that the conversation he was having was with his "connection," or dealer. This guy was trying to score! Within minutes, as I was pumping my gas, a car pulled up to the side of the station. The guy who had been on the phone ran over to the driver, jumped in the car where he stayed for less than a minute, got out, scurried to another vehicle, and quickly drove off. Both people drove away from the station at approximately the same time. In my mind, I had just witnessed what I suspected all along. An addict has just "connected" and was now on his way to get high. What happened next was truly frightening. With no effort or control on my part whatsoever, it seemed as if my whole world changed in an instant. Suddenly, I was the Chuck I had been for many years. Suddenly, I was an addict that needed heroin. Plus, I was broke, desperate, and wondering where I could steal something to get enough money to buy some dope. Amazed and very conscious of what was taking place, I vigorously shook my head like a dog that gets soaked with water, and went on my way.

One last comment about the relationship between behavior and an individual's self-concept: Over the years I have known many people who came into NA, stayed clean for awhile, then reverted to their old lifestyles. After using drugs again for various amounts of time, some return to meetings with the hopes of getting their lives back together. These people almost always say that the fun they used to have getting high was ruined by their previous participation in the program. Commonly, they will say, "There's nothing worse than a head full of NA and a body full of dope."

From everything I've been able to observe, our ghosts really affect the process of change. For those of us who "make it" and for those of us who do not—the tension between our old and new selves, which does seem to decrease over time, continues. If we are lucky, the masks we developed as convicts and addicts gradually disappear. If we have the motivation, sense of purpose, opportunity, and support, we sometimes get to replace them with faces of hope, love, and compassion.

CONCLUDING THOUGHTS

The stories of the fellas, as well as the experiences of the untold millions who experience the effects of the negative cultural conceptions of heroin and other illegal drugs, are far from over. The idea that drugs are dangerous and users need to be imprisoned or sent to treatment (or both) is seldom questioned. It affected the way I was defined in court the last time I got sentenced and is an impression that continues to be bolstered in political arenas and the popular culture today. That most people who use drugs, illegal or not, live normal lives is so far removed from the cultural consciousness that to even make such a statement is analogous to blasphemy for the deeply religious. Within the context of the morally, politically, and economically driven War on Drugs, people who use illegal drugs are perceived as threatening. Therefore, they need to be identified, isolated, treated and/or incarcerated, and cured.

Sentiments against the drug war have been building for years. Partly because of the efforts of thousands who have been pushing for more sensible drug policies, as well as the economic downswing this country has undergone since September 11, 2001, the tide does seem to be changing—a little. In November 2000, California voters passed Proposition 36, a bill that basically makes it illegal to incarcerate low-level drug offenders without offering them treatment first. Before passage of Proposition 36, the California Legislative Analyst's Office projected that, if passed, the bill would save $100–150 million in prison costs annually and divert as many as 36,000 new prisoners and probation and parole violators to treatment programs annually. Several states, strapped because of budget constraints, are reducing mandatory minimum sentencing guidelines for drug law violations, closing down penal facilities, cutting jobs for prison personnel, and reforming parole guidelines (Greene and Schiraldi, 2002). At the same time, drug war propaganda continues. Since the "War on Terrorism" started, we are seeing government-sponsored television commercials informing us that anyone who purchases illegal drugs is a supporter of terror. Clearly, we still have a long way to go.

Ethan Nadelmann, director of the Drug Policy Alliance, offers a powerful vision that can help guide us toward a different, more sane future:

Imagine . . . a policy that starts by acknowledging that drugs are here to stay, and that we have no choice but to learn how to live with them so that they cause the least possible harm. Imagine a policy that focuses on reducing not illicit drug use per se but the crime and misery caused by both drug abuse and prohibitionist policies. And imagine a drug policy based not on the fear, prejudice, and ignorance that drive America's current approach but rather on common sense, science, public health concerns, and human rights. (Nadelmann, 1998)

Incarcerating addicts, as the fellas have helped us see, produces regulars. Though not all who spend time in prison become regulars, many do. Besides, incarceration generally has negative effects on even those who are the least prisonized. Being socialized in this manner is *the* criminogenic effect of prison and inner-city neighborhoods and arguably one of the greatest harms created by the drug war. It is an outlook that acts as a means of survival and is related to the lack of opportunities for legal resources in both environments. It is not that prisons teach more about crime. It is not that people in inner-city neighborhoods get involved in criminal activity because they have flawed characters, deviant psyches, or pathological personalities. Rather, the way individuals evaluate themselves within these social worlds aids in the development of a perspective that defines as normal actions interpreted as deviant by the mainstream culture. It is a perspective that allows the holder, who often exists within a world of deprivation, lack, and ostracization, a sense of respect and dignity in his or her own eyes and in the eyes of peers.

As a final comment, I feel it important to point out there are many "fellas" in society, in the criminal justice system, and in the making. The story of those presented here, however, compared with others with similar backgrounds, is extraordinary. Their life histories portray the social forces that helped shape the way they saw themselves and the world, and what they had to go through to alter the directions of their lives. As such, they are extreme examples that highlight the process of individual change. As well as pointing to what *should not* be done in social policy, they show us that even those defined as being the highest "risk" or the most incorrigible are capable of change.

Appendix

A Bit More About the Research and Methodology

ACCESS: FINDING THE FELLAS

Because of my own affiliation with NA, I personally knew several of the fellas at the time I began the interviewing process. These personal acquaintances, or what might be called a convenience sample, were my first respondents. They, in turn, led me to others who fit the criteria of the study.[1] Still, obstacles to locating the number of men I was looking for arose. For example, I knew, or knew others who knew, several ex-drug users who had been to prison, but the drug they used was not heroin. There were others who had used heroin but did not do time in prison.

Once I found a potential respondent, I briefly explained what I was trying to do and wondered if he would be willing to help. I talked about being in school and doing research about the lives of people who had used heroin, been to prison, and were now clean. I mentioned how difficult it was finding guys with this type of background. Most often, this brought about a smile and a sense of understanding. The response I received was, generally, very positive. None of the men I asked told me they would not be willing to help. As it turned out, however, two never seemed to find the time for an interview.

---

[1] For information on convenience samples or snowball sampling (asking known respondents to identify others who might be willing to participate), see Maxfield and Babbie, 1995.

DATA COLLECTION: INTERVIEWS

The bulk of the data in this book came from interviewing the fellas during a six-month period in 1998. There were a few times when I would be eating in a restaurant, driving in a car, or sitting in a 12-step meeting with one of them and something relevant to this study was mentioned. On these occasions, I took notes about the content of the conversation as soon as possible.

Once someone agreed to an interview, it was necessary to set up a time and place to meet. To accomplish this, I always did my best to accommodate the fellas. We met in each other's homes, parks, in a back office where my wife worked, or at places of employment. One, who owns his own business, let me interview him in his office. Another, who does counseling work for people with HIV, had me meet him at his job after work. Still another, who worked at a walk-in sobriety center in conjunction with a local police department, let me interview him while he was working.

Obtaining a completed interview was not always as simple as just meeting with someone at an agreed upon place and time and getting it done. There were cases where it was necessary to meet with one of them two or three times. In these instances, the interviews were usually four hours or longer and the time had to be broken up to fit their schedules.

The interviews, which were recorded on audiotape, took from roughly two to five hours each to complete. They all followed a similar format but were based on mostly open-ended questions. I began each one by explaining that I was looking for times over the course of their lives when changes took place that affected how each man saw himself and his world.

Once the basic overview of what I was looking for was laid out, I asked them to tell me about themselves with an emphasis on turning points, starting from when they were children. By telling their stories in this longitudinal manner, I was able to see which events and situations were most important to them over time. Moreover, I was able to see how their lives unfolded as a process of change. Once they began telling their stories, I asked further questions, probing deeper into potentially informative areas to guide the direction of the dialogue. Questions I asked were always raised with the intention of gaining more information about how they perceived the particular issue being discussed and how it related to their self-concepts. It was often the case that they went on tangents that had nothing to do with the topic, and I gently returned them to my sought-after theme.

There were times when they touched on a specific situation or event and quickly moved on as if it had nothing to do with how they changed over time. For example, one might mention getting arrested and jailed for the first time and immediately go on to something else that happened later in his life. Here, I would ask him to talk a little more about that first arrest, that first experience in jail, and how it made him feel at the time, and what it was like for him after he got out. Often, as he went into greater detail about a specific situation, more was revealed about how the experience affected the way he saw himself over time.

As the interviews progressed in number, I began to notice distinct differences in the way the fellas talked about their lives. Several clearly understood the idea of a self-concept, easily grasped the process I was looking for, used narratives placing themselves within a larger social context, and provided intelligent, insightful answers. In contrast, others seemed almost lifeless and required a constant, but gentle push to open up. Interviewing them was a strain. Getting them to speak made me think of what it must be like for a dentist to have to extract teeth from a scared patient. There were yet others who were very responsive, but unable to grasp what I was after. Regardless of my efforts, the idea of a self-concept never seemed to register for them and, therefore, telling their story from the perspective of how they saw themselves was impossible. For instance, one may have told me about a period in his life where he was not using heroin, where he was out of prison, living with a woman, and doing good. After hearing this I might ask, as I did with all the men on occasion, "and how did you see yourself at that time? How do you think others saw you?" The typical response was "I don't know. I never thought about it."[2] This last type often told his story in chronological order by focusing on arrests and prison commitments as major turning points in his life. Taken as a whole, all the interviews were rich in detail and provided fruitful data.

Nothing was offered to any of the men as pay for their time. Whether I knew an individual beforehand or not, by the time an interview took place he had a rough idea who I was, where I've been, and what I was doing. In short, the men saw me as one of them. It is possible to say that we, as a group, tend to see ourselves as survivors, as people who have a story to tell. Such a perspective is enhanced by participating in 12-step programs, which revolve around storytelling (Denzin, 1987). Part of the 12-step ideology has to do with helping others, lending your hand to the addict who still suffers, and doing what you can to give rather than take. This common background and way of thinking seemed to have a lot to do with getting the fellas to cooperate. In fact, most of them seemed eager to do so.

PARTICIPANT PROTECTION

All participation in this study was voluntary. Measures were taken to protect the men from any harm that might have taken place as a result of their cooperation. During interviews, some past criminal activity was disclosed. This could have posed a threat to an individual if, for example, a law-enforcement agency took interest in the data.

To ensure the men's protection, their names and the areas where they lived will not be disclosed. All participant observation notes as well as the audiotaped interviews were quickly made devoid of names. In addition, once collected,

---

[2] This is consistent with the idea that human beings do not generally think about their own self-concept unless they are in unusual, often uncomfortable situations that make them self-conscious (Shibutani, 1991, 90).

the data from the tapes were transcribed as soon as possible. Once transcribed, the tapes were destroyed.

None of the fellas were, to my knowledge, in a "phase of active addiction." That is, they were not currently using either drugs or alcohol. This reduced the likelihood of them being suspected of criminal activity at the time of the interviews. Nevertheless, to ensure their protection, any discussion of past criminal activity was kept to an abstract level. All interviews and interaction with the fellas began by me strongly suggesting that no specific, legally identifiable information be disclosed. As it turned out, none was.

WHY ONLY CLEAN MALE HEROIN ADDICTS WHO HAVE BEEN TO PRISON?

Women were excluded from this study for several reasons. First, the fact that more men are sent to prison than women made the sample easier to locate. Second, and more importantly, men and women are treated differently based on the way they are seen in the popular culture. This, in turn, affects how they see themselves and their behavior. The inclusion of women would have broadened the scope of the project in data collection and analysis beyond the limited time and resources that were available.

For similar reasons I sought only heroin users because they see themselves differently than do people who use other drugs. For instance, they typically see and refer to users of "speed" as if they were a breed apart from themselves because of the erratic behavior that stems from doing things such as staying awake and not eating for long periods. Likewise, "speed freaks" often look at individuals who use heroin as junkies or real addicts, as people who are more criminal and prone to danger. By focusing only on men with histories of heroin addiction, I narrowed the topic and increased both the feasibility and quality of the study.

To study the process of identity transformation, I sought people who were clean rather than those who were still using drugs. Focusing on people who were clean also made the project more feasible. If anyone I interviewed was using illegal drugs he would, by definition, be breaking the law. Being around illegal activity could have endangered my own well-being because I am an ex-heroin user who has been legally categorized as a person who could be tried under the California three strikes law.

STUDY LIMITATIONS AND STRENGTHS

The answers I was seeking had a lot to do with my own story—with trying to explain what happened to me. In a way then, this study can be seen as an autoethnography that has to do with the researcher possessing an "often permanent self-identification with a group and full internal membership, as recognized both by themselves and the people of whom they are a part" (Hayano, 1979, 100). Because of my personal history, the interpretation of the data reflects the vantage point of a recovering addict who has served many years in prison. Therefore, my involvement can be seen as a two-edged sword that likely had positive and negative effects on the research.

A problem I encountered because of my familiarity with the topic had to do with failing to probe into certain areas during the interview process. Because the men knew of my background and we used similar language, they in many instances assumed (and rightly so) that I knew what they meant about certain meanings. For example, the issue of "kicking" (going through withdrawals) in jail might have come up and instead of telling me what it was like (knowing I knew), the individual might just move on with his story. At these times, if I had the presence of mind to do so, I would interrupt and ask him to go into more detail because I needed to know his view.

Another issue that may have biased the research had to do with the way the men saw me as a person. Their statements may have been influenced by a desire to appear a certain way in my presence and to please me. In other words, they might have chosen what to say to look and sound good. Because one of them perceived me as someone who had been to prison, for example, it is doubtful he would tell me anything about cooperating with police by informing on others so he could stay out of jail. Such behavior is taboo in both prisons and illegal drug using cultures. As it happened, not one man mentioned such activity. Given the rewards offered by police for "snitching" in drug-related cases today, it would seem plausible to assume that some of them "cooperated" at some point in their lives.

One of the dilemmas about this study had to do with the men looking back in their lives and talking about things that happened long ago. In doing so, they may have reinterpreted what actually happened based on their current views. For example, when I was 20 years old, I was arrested for burglary. That is a fact. Back then it meant I got caught and had to go to jail. Today I regret the act, feel bad about what I did, and see it as an unfortunate event that has much greater meaning than whether or not I got caught. Though the issue of retrospection can be seen as a weakness of the method, it is also a strength because such re-definitions of situations reflect changing self-concepts.

My closeness to the fellas and the topic gave me many advantages. That they thought of me in a way similar to the way they saw themselves allowed for a relatively open dialogue. My having "been there," to places and situations "that only we have been," allowed for a sense of trust that might have been impossible for an outsider to obtain. "[T]he auto-ethnographer has several obvious practical advantages . . . prior knowledge of the native language . . . feelings of empathy and emotions which insiders share from knowing their subjects on a deep, subtle level" (Hayano, 1979, 101).

Perhaps the greatest advantage I had was my ability to talk to these men in their own language, which generally deviated from the mainstream norm. "Indeed, it is a mark of membership in the group to be able to use and understand the group's jargon" (Lutz, 1989, 5; for the use of argot among criminal narcotic addicts, see Maurer, 1981). The vocabulary I was able to use as I spent time with them acted as a powerful symbol, the use of which helped me gain not only access into their lives but information that might have otherwise been impossible to uncover. In short, my use of addict/prison language during conversations and interviews I had with the fellas set up situations where I was not seen so much as someone doing a formal interview (like a counselor or parole officer) but, rather, as someone they could relate to, feel comfortable with, and trust.

Much of the dialogue that took place between us was more like a conversation than an interview. Oftentimes, information disclosed by one of them triggered memories of a similar experience from my own life which I, in turn, would talk about. At times, this had the effect of increasing the depth of the interview for it helped generate new thoughts and questions that might otherwise have never come up. Disclosing things about myself also increased both the level of trust and bond between us.

The fact that the stories of these men were probably accurate reflections of their lives is an inherent strength of the project. Their honesty and willingness to participate had a lot to do with their perception of me as someone who has shared similar experiences. However, their accounts may not be representative of all male heroin addicts who have spent time in prison because they were a small, self-selected group of individuals from southern California.

Bibliography

Alcoholics Anonymous. 1976. New York: Alcoholics Anonymous World Services.

Anderson, Elijah. 1999. *Code of the Street: Decency, Violence, and the Moral Life of the Inner City.* New York: Norton.

Anslinger, Harry, & Cooper, Courtney R. 1937, July. "Marijuana: Assassin of Youth." *American Magazine:* 18–19, 150–153.

Athens, Lonnie H. 1995. "Dramatic Self Change." *Sociological Quarterly,* 36(3): 571–586.

Austin, James, & Irwin, John. 2001. *It's About Time: America's Imprisonment Binge.* Belmont, California: Wadsworth.

Ausubel, David P. 1952. "An Evaluation of Recent Adolescent Drug Addiction." *Mental Hygiene,* 36: 373–382.

Bacon, G., Richard Boardman, Spencer Coxe, Caleb Foote, James V. Giles, David Greenberg, Mike Ingerman, John Irwin, Alex Knopp, Sam Legg, Jan Marinissen, Edwin C. Morgenroth, Tom Nelson, George Sawyer, Jane Schulman, & Mark Morris. 1971. *Struggle for Justice: A Report on Crime and Punishment in America.* New York: Hill and Wang.

Bailey, Pierce. 1916. "The Heroin Habit." *New Republic,* 6: 314–316.

Baum, Dan. 1996. *Smoke and Mirrors: The War on Drugs and The Politics of Failure.* Boston: Back Bay Books.

Bayer, Ronald. 1981. "Crime, Punishment and the Decline of Liberal Optimism." *Crime and Delinquency,* 27: 169–190.

Becker, Howard S. 1963. *Outsiders: Studies in the Sociology of Deviance.* New York: Free Press.

Beckett, Katherine, & Sasson, Theodore. 2000. *The Politics of Injustice: Crime and Punishment in America.* Thousand Oaks, California: Pine Forge Press.

Biernacki, Patrick. 1979. "Junkie Work, 'Hustles' and Social Status Among Heroin Addicts." *Journal of Drug Issues,* 9: 535–551.

———. 1986. *Pathways from Heroin Addiction: Recovery Without Treatment.* Philadelphia: Temple University Press.

Bishop, Ernest S. 1912. "Morphinism and Its Treatment." *Journal of the American Medical Association,* 58: 1499–1504.

Blumer, Herbert. 1969. *Symbolic Interactionism: Perspective and Method.* Englewood Cliffs, New Jersey: Prentice-Hall.

Bourgois, Philippe. 1995. *In Search of Respect: Selling Crack in El Barrio.* Cambridge, Massachusetts: Cambridge University Press.

Brill, Leon. 1972. *The De-Addiction Process: Studies in the De-Addiction of Confirmed Heroin Addicts.* Springfield, Illinois: Charles C Thomas.

Brown, Claude. 1965. *Manchild in the Promised Land,* 10th edition. New York: Signet Books.

Bush, George. 1990. *Public Papers of the Presidents of the United States: George Bush, 1989.* Washington, D.C., Government Printing Office.

Butterfield, Fox. 2000, November 29. "Often, Parole Is One Stop on the Way Back to Prison." *New York Times,* A1.

Chambliss, William J. 1999. *Power, Politics and Crime.* Boulder, Colorado: Westview Press.

Charmaz, Kathy. 1991. *Good Days, Bad Days: The Self in Chronic Illness and Time.* New Brunswick, New Jersey: Rutgers University Press.

Clear, Todd R., Rose, Dina R., & Ryder, Judith A. 2001. "Incarceration and the Community: The Problem of Removing and Returning Offenders." *Crime and Delinquency,* 47(3): 335–351.

Clemmer, Donald. 1940. *The Prison Community.* New York: Holt, Rinehart, and Winston.

Coleman, James W. 1975. *Addiction, Crime and Abstinence: An Investigation of Addict Behavior.* Unpublished dissertation: University of California Santa Barbara.

Conrad, Peter, & Schneider, Joseph W. 1992. *Deviance and Medicalization: From Badness to Sickness.* Philadelphia: Temple University Press.

Cooley, Charles H. 1996. "The Social Self." In Henry Pontell (ed), *Social Deviance: Readings in Theory and Research.* Englewood Cliffs, New Jersey: Prentice Hall, 63–64.

Coombs, Robert H. 1981. "Drug Abuse as Career." *Journal of Drug Issues,* 11: 369–387.

Courtwright, David T. 1978. "Opiate Addiction as a Consequence of the Civil War." *Journal of Civil War History,* 24: 101–111.

———. 1982. *Dark Paradise: Opiate Addiction in America Before 1940.* Cambridge, Massachusetts: Harvard University Press.

Courtwright, David, Joseph, Herman, & Des Jarlais, Don. 1989. *Addicts Who Survived.* Knoxville: University of Tennessee Press.

Crawford, Gail A., Washington, Melvin C., & Senay, Edward C. 1983. "Careers with Heroin." *International Journal of the Addictions,* 18(5): 701–715.

Crothers, Thomas D. 1900. "Morphinism Among Physicians." *Current Literature: A Magazine of Contemporary Record,* 27(1): 46.

Denzin, Norman K. 1987. *The Recovering Alcoholic.* Beverly Hills, California: Sage.

———. 1987a. *Treating Alcoholism: An Alcoholics Anonymous Approach.* Newbury Park, California: Sage.

De Quincey, Thomas. [1821] 1966. *Confessions of an English Opium-Eater and Other Writings.* New York: New American Library.

DiClemente, Carlo C. 1994. *Can Personality Change?* Washington, D.C.: American Psychological Association.

Durkheim, Émile. [1893] 1964. *The Division of Labor in Society.* New York: Free Press.

Ebaugh, Helen R. 1988. *Becoming an Ex: The Process of Role Exit.* Chicago: University of Chicago Press.

Faupel, Charles E., & Klockars, Carl B. 1987. "Drugs-Crime Connections: Elaborations from the Life Histories of Hard-Core Heroin Addicts." *Social Problems,* 34(1): 54–68.

Fromm, Erich. 1976. *To Have or To Be.* New York: Harper and Row.

Garfinkel, Harold. 1956. "Conditions of Successful Degradation Ceremonies." *American Journal of Sociology,* 61(5): 420–424.

"Getting Straight." 1999, March 9. Narrator Cokie Roberts. *ABC Nightline,* New York.

Goffman, Erving. 1963. *Stigma: Notes on the Management of Spoiled Identity.* Englewood Cliffs, New Jersey: Prentice-Hall.

Goldman, Abigail. 1998, March, 20. "Robert Downey Ordered to Spend 3 Extra Days in Jail." *Los Angeles Times,* B-3.

Gottfredson, Michael R., & Hirschi, Travis. 1990. *A General Theory of Crime.* Stanford, California: Stanford University Press.

Greene, Judith, & Schiraldi, Vincent. 2002. *Cutting Correctly: New Prison Policies for Times of Fiscal Crisis.* Washington, D.C.: Justice Policy Institute.

Gusfield, Joseph R. 1986. *Symbolic Crusade: Status Politics and the American Temperance Movement,* 2nd edition. Chicago: University of Illinois Press.

Hagan, John, & Coleman, Petty Juleigh. 2001. "Returning Captives of the American War on Drugs: Issues of Community and Family Reentry." *Crime and Delinquency,* 47(3): 352–367.

Harper's Bazaar. 1901, February 2. "Concerning Temperance and Society; An Editorial Comment."

Harre, Rom. 1998. *The Singular Self: An Introduction to the Psychology of Personhood.* London: Sage.

Hayano, Dan. M. 1979. "Auto-Ethnography: Paradigms, Problems, and Prospects." *Human Organization: Journal of the Society for Applied Anthropology,* 38(1): 99–104.

Herrnstein, Richard J., & Wilson, James Q. 1985. *Crime and Human Nature.* New York: Simon and Schuster.

Hser, Yih-ing, Hoffman, Valerie, Grella, Christine E., & Douglas, Anglin M. 2001. "A 33 Year Follow Up of Narcotics Addicts." *Archives of General Psychiatry,* 58(5): 503–508.

Hull, J. M. 1885. "The Opium Habit [in Iowa]." *Iowa State Board of Health, Third Biennial Report.* Des Moines: George. E. Roberts, 535–545.

Human Rights Watch. 2000, June. *Punishment and Prejudice: Racial Disparities in the War on Drugs.* New York.

Irwin, John. 1970. *The Felon.* Englewood Cliffs, New Jersey: Prentice-Hall.

———. 1980. *Prisons in Turmoil.* Boston: Little, Brown.

Irwin, John, & Cressey, Donald R. 1962. "Thieves, Convicts and the Inmate Culture." *Social Problems,* 10(2): 142–155.

Irwin, John, Schiraldi, Vincent, & Ziedenberg, Jason. *America's One Million Non-Violent Prisoners.* 1999. Washington, D.C.: Justice Policy Institute.

Jacobs, Jerry. 1969. *The Search for Help: A Study of the Retarded Child in the Community.* New York: Brunner/Mazel.

Johnson, Robert. 1996. *Hard Time: Understanding and Reforming the Prison,* 2nd edition. Belmont, California: Wadsworth.

Jones, Richard S., & Schmid, Thomas J. 2000. *Doing Time: Prison Experience and Identity Among First-Time Inmates.* Stamford, Connecticut: JAI.

Jouet, Daniel. 1883. *Étude Sur le Morphinisme Chronique.* These de Paris.

Kane, Francis F. 1917. "Drugs and Crime." *Journal of the American Institute of Criminal Law,* 8: 502–517.

Katz, Jack. 1988. *Seductions of Crime: Moral and Sensual Attractions in Doing Evil.* New York: Basic Books.

Katz, Jesse. 2000, February 15. "A Nation of Too Many Prisoners?" *Los Angeles Times,* A1.

Kolb, Lawrence. 1925. "Types and Characteristics of Drug Addicts." *Mental Hygiene,* 9(2): 300–313.

Landry, Mim J. 1994. *Understanding Drugs of Abuse: The Process of Addiction, Treatment and Recovery.* Washington, D.C.: American Psychiatric Press.

Lathrop, George Parson. 1880. "The Sorcery of Madjoon." *Scribner's Monthly: An Illustrated Magazine for the People,* 20: 416–422.

Layard, James Coulter. 1874. "Morphine." *Atlantic Monthly: A Magazine of Literature, Science, Art and Politics,* 33(195): 697–712.

Lee, Martin A., & Shlain, Bruce. 1985. *Acid Dreams: The Complete Social History of LSD, the CIA, the Sixties and Beyond.* New York: Grove Weidenfeld.

Leet, Duane A., Rush, George E., & Smith, Anthony M. 1997. *Gangs, Graffiti and Violence: A Realistic Guide to the Scope and Nature of Gangs in America.* Incline Village, Nevada: Copperhouse.

Lemert, Edwin M. 1996. "Primary and Secondary Deviation." In Henry N. Pontell (ed), *Social Deviance: Readings in Theory and Research,* 2nd edition. New Jersey: Prentice-Hall.

Lichtenstein, Perry M. 1914. "Narcotic Addiction." *New York Medical Journal,* 100: 962–966.

Lindesmith, Alfred R. 1968. *Addiction and Opiates.* Chicago: Aldine.

Literary Digest. 1920, March 6. "What is Back of the Drug Habit?" 64: 27–28.

Lofland, John. 1966. *Doomsday Cult: A Study of Conversion, Proselytization, and Maintenance of Faith.* Englewood Cliffs, New Jersey: Prentice Hall.

Lutz, William. 1989. *Beyond Nineteen Eighty-Four: Doublespeak in a Post-Orwellian Age.* Urbana, Illinois: National Council of Teachers in English.

Maguire, Kathleen, & Pastore, Ann L. (eds). 1999. *Sourcebook of Criminal Justice Statistics 1996.* U.S. Department of Justice, Bureau of Justice Statistics. Washington, D.C.: USGPO.

Manchester, Lee. 1995. Letter to the author.

Mark, Tami L., Woody, George E., Juday, Tim, & Kleber, Herbert D. 2001. "The Economic Costs of Heroin Addiction in the United States." *Drug and Alcohol Dependence,* 61(2): 195–206.

Maruna, Shadd. 1997. "Going Straight: Desistance from Crime and Self-narratives of Reform." *Narrative Study of Lives,* 5: 59–93.

———. 2001. *Making Good: How Ex-Convicts Reform and Rebuild Their Lives.* Washington, D.C.: American Psychological Association.

Matza, David. 1964. *Delinquency and Drift.* New York: John Wiley and Sons.

Mauer, Marc. 1999. *Race to Incarcerate: The Sentencing Project.* New York: New Press.

Maughs, Sydney. 1941. " A Concept of Psychopathy and Psychopathic Personality: Its Evolution and Historical Development." *Journal of Criminal Psychopathology,* 2(3): 330–356, 465–499.

Maurer, David W. 1981. *Language of the Underworld.* Lexington: University of Kentucky Press.

Maxfield, Michael G., & Babbie, Earl. 1995. *Research Methods for Criminal Justice and Criminology.* Belmont, California: Wadsworth.

McCorkle, Lloyd, & Korn, Richard. 1954. "Resocialization Within Prison Walls." *Annals of the American Academy of Political and Social Science,* 293: 88–98.

McGuire, Frank A. & Lichtenstein, Perry M. 1916. "The Drug Habit." *Medical Record,* 90: 185–191.

Miller, Jerome. 1996. *Search and Destroy: African-American Males in the Criminal Justice System.* Cambridge: Cambridge University Press.

Miller, Richard L. 1996. *Drug Warriors and Their Prey: From Police Power to Police State.* Westport, Connecticut: Praeger.

Moffitt, Terrie E. 1993. "Adolescence-Limited and Life-Course-Persistent Antisocial Behavior: A Developmental Taxonomy." *Psychological Review,* 100(4): 674–701.

Morgan, Wayne H. 1974. *Yesterday's Addicts: American Society and Drug Abuse, 1865–1920.* Norman: University of Oklahoma Press.

———. 1981. *Drugs in America: A Social History, 1800–1980.* Syracuse, New York: Syracuse University Press.

Musto, David F. 1971. "The American Antinarcotic Movement: Clinical Research and Public Policy." *Clinical Research,* 19: 601–605.

———. 1973. *The American Disease: Origins of Narcotic Control.* New York: Oxford University Press.

Nadelmann, Ethan. 1998, January. "A Commonsense Drug Policy." *Foreign Affairs:* 111–126.

Narcotics Anonymous, 5th edition. 1982. Van Nuys, California: World Services Office.

Newsweek. April 21, 1969. "The Drug Generation: Growing Younger."

New York Times. 1877, December 30. "The Opium Habits Power: Its Extent in the United States," p. 8.

———. 1881, February, 21. "Topics in the Sagebrush: The Chinese Treaties in the Nevada Legislature," P1(7).

———. 1951, February 8. "Stiffer Law Asked in Narcotics Cases." P18(2).

———. 1956, January 10. "Death Demanded for Heroin Sales." P12(1).

Norris, Mikki, Conrad, Chris, & Resner, Virginia. 1998. *Shattered Lives: Portraits from America's Drug War.* El Cerrito, California: Creative Xpressions.

Parenti, Christian. 1999. *Lockdown America: Police and Prisons in the Age of Crisis.* London: Verso.

Parsons, Deborah C., & Jesilow, Paul. 2001. *In the Same Voice.* Santa Ana, California: Seven Locks Press.

Peteet, John R. 1993. "A Closer Look at the Role of a Spiritual Approach in Addictions Treatment." *Journal of Substance Abuse Treatment,* 10: 263–267.

Peyrot, Mark. 1985. "Narcotics Anonymous: Its History, Structure, and Approach." *International Journal of the Addictions,* 20(10): 1509–1522.

Quinney, Richard. 1970. *The Social Reality of Crime.* Boston: Little, Brown.

Rasor, Robert W. 1972. "The United States Public Health Service Institutional Treatment Program for Narcotics Addicts at Lexington, Kentucky." In Leon Brill & Louis Lieberman (eds), *Major Modalities in the Treatment of Drug Abuse*. New York: Behavioral Publications.

Reagan, Ronald. 1991. *Public Papers of the Presidents of the United States: Ronald Reagan, 1988*. Washington, D.C., Government Printing Office.

Richards, Stephan C. 1995. *The Structure of Prison Release: An Extended Case Study of Prison Release, Work Release, and Parole*. New York: McGraw-Hill.

Roberts, Steven V. 1988, March 1. "Mrs. Reagan Assails Drug Users." *New York Times,* A16.

Robins, Lee N. 1973. "A Followup of Vietnam Drug Users." *Special Action Office Monograph Series A,* No. 1. Washington, D.C.: Executive Office of the President.

Ronel, Natti. 1998. "Narcotics Anonymous: Understanding the 'Bridge of Recovery.'" *Journal of Offender Rehabilitation,* 27: 179–197.

Rosenbaum, Marsha. 1981. *Women on Heroin*. New Brunswick, New Jersey: Rutgers University Press.

Sampson, Robert J., & Laub, John H. 1993. *Crime in the Making: Pathways and Turning Points Through Life*. Cambridge, Massachusetts: Harvard University Press.

Sandmeyer, Elmer Clarence. 1939. *The Anti-Chinese Movement in California*. Urbana: University of Illinois Press.

Sceleth, Charles E., & Kuh, Sydney. 1924. "Drug Addiction." *Journal of the American Medical Association,* 82(9): 679–682.

Schiraldi, Vincent, Holman, Barry, & Beatty, Phillip. 2000. *Poor Prescription: The Cost of Imprisoning Drug Offenders in the United States*. San Francisco: Justice Policy Institute.

Schmid, Thomas J., & Jones, Richard S. 1991. "Suspended Identity: Identity Transformation in a Maximum Security Prison." *Symbolic Interaction,* 14(4): 415–432.

———. 1993. "Ambivalent Actions: Prison Adaptation Strategies of First-Time, Short-Term Inmates." *Journal of Contemporary Ethnography,* 21(4): 439–463.

Science Digest. 1952, November. "True Drug Addicts," 33–34.

Shelden, Randall G., Tracy, Sharon K., & Brown, William B. 2001. *Youth Gangs in American Society*. Belmont, California: Wadsworth.

Shepherd, William G. 1923, November 30. "Youth + Dope = Crime." *American Legion Weekly:* 7, 8, 23, 24.

Shibutani, Tamotsu. 1972. "Reference Groups as Perspectives." In Howard Shapiro and Robert Gliner (eds), *Human Perspectives: Introductory Readings for Sociology*. New York: Free Press, 15–25.

———. 1986. *Social Processes: An Introduction to Sociology*. Berkeley: University of California Press.

———. 1991. *Society and Personality: An Interactionist Approach to Social Psychology,* 2nd edition. New Brunswick: Transaction.

Shover, Neil. 1985. *Aging Criminals*. Beverly Hills, California: Sage.

Sloman, Larry. 1979. *The History of Marijuana in America: Reefer Madness*. New York: Bobbs-Merrill.

Snow, Michael. 1973. "Maturing Out of Narcotic Addiction in New York City." *International Journal of the Addictions,* 8(6): 921–938.

Stall, Robb, & Biernacki, Patrick. 1986. "Spontaneous Remission from the Problematic Use of Substances: An Inductive Model Derived from a Comparative Analysis of the

Alcohol, Opiate, Tobacco, and Food/Obesity Literatures." *International Journal of the Addictions,* 21(1): 1–23.

Sterne, Albert E. 1905. "Have Drug Addictions a Pathologic Basis?" *Journal of the American Medical Association,* 44: 609–612.

Stone, Bob. 1997. *My Years with Narcotics Anonymous.* Hulon Pendleton Publishing.

Strauss, Anselm. 1969. *Mirrors and Masks: The Search for Identity.* San Francisco, California: Sociology Press.

Sutherland, Edwin H. 1939. *Principles of Criminology,* 3rd edition. Philadelphia: Lippencott.

Sykes, Gresham M., & Matza, David. 1957. "Techniques of Neutralization: A Theory of Delinquency." *American Sociological Review,* 22: 664–670.

Tannenbaum, Frank. 1938. *Crime and the Community.* Boston: Ginn.

Terry, Charles E. 1920a. "Narcotic Drug Addiction and Rational Administration." *American Medicine,* 26: 29–35.

———. 1920b. "Report of Committee on Habit Forming Drugs." *American Journal of Public Health,* 10(1): 83–86.

———. 1921. "Symposium on Narcotic Drug Addiction: Some Recent Experiments in Narcotic Control." *American Journal of Public Health,* 11(1): 32–44.

Terry, Charles E., & Pellens, Mildred [1928] 1970. *The Opium Problem.* Montclair, New Jersey: Patterson Smith.

Terry, Charles M. 1997. "The Function of Humor in Prison." *Journal of Contemporary Criminal Justice,* 13(1): 23–40.

———. 2000. "Beyond Punishment: Perpetuating Difference From the Prison Experience." *Humanity and Society,* 24(2): 108–135.

Time Magazine. 1937, February 15. "Narcotic Farm No. 2." 27: 69–70.

Travis, Jeremy, Solomon, Amy L., & Waul, Michelle. 2001. *From Prison to Home: The Dimensions and Consequences of Prisoner Reentry.* Washington, D.C.: Urban Institute.

Trevino, Javier A. 1992. "Alcoholics Anonymous as Durkheimian Religion." *Research in the Social Scientific Study of Religion,* 4: 183–208.

Trice, Harrison M., & Roman, Paul M. 1978. "Delabeling, Relabeling, and Alcoholics Anonymous." In Earl Rubington and Martin S. Weinberg (eds), *Deviance: The Interactionist Perspective,* 3rd edition. New York: Macmillan.

Vaillant, George E. 1983. *The Natural History of Alcoholism.* Cambridge, Massachusetts: Harvard University Press.

Vigil, James Diego. 1988. *Barrio Gangs: Street Life and Identity in Southern California.* Austin: University of Texas Press, Austin.

Waldorf, Dan. 1970. "Life Without Heroin: Some Social Adjustments During Long-term Periods of Voluntary Abstention." *Social Problems,* 18(2): 229–243.

Walker, Samuel. 2001. *Sense and Nonsense About Crime and Drugs,* 4th edition. Belmont, California: Wadsworth.

Wallis, Frederic A. 1925. "Menace of the Drug Addict." *Current History,* 21: 740–743.

Weber, Max. 1958. *The Protestant Ethic and the Spirit of Capitalism.* New York: Scribner's.

Winick, Charles. 1962. "Maturing Out of Narcotics Addiction." *U.N. Bulletin on Narcotics,* 14: 1–7.

Wood, Daniel B. 1997. "To Keep Peace, Prisons Allow Race to Rule." *Christian Science Monitor,* September 16.

Yablonsky, Lewis. 1965. *The Tunnel Back.* New York: Macmillan.